DEADLY FIGHTING SKILLS
OF THE WORLD

St. Martin's Griffin
New York

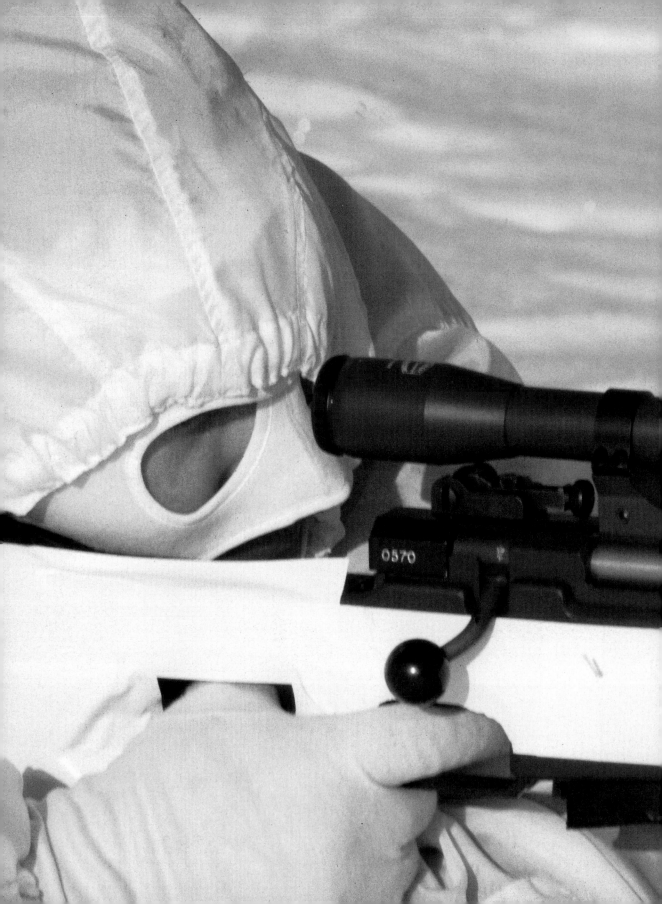

DEADLY FIGHTING SKILLS OF THE WORLD

STEVE CRAWFORD

First published in Great Britain in 1997
by Sidgwick & Jackson Limited
A division of Macmillan General Books

THOMAS DUNNE BOOKS.
An imprint of St. Martin's Press. All rights reserved. Printed in Italy.

ISBN 0-312-20262-8

First U.S. Edition 1999

Editorial and Design:
Brown Packaging Books Limited
Bradley's Close, 74-77 White Lion Street
London N1 9PF

This book is for informational purposes only. It is not intended for use
as a training manual of any kind. Readers should not use any of the
unarmed combat or other military techniques described in this book
for any purpose whatsoever.

PICTURE CREDITS
Military Picture Library: 19, 28, 36, 37, 50-51, 60-61, 71, 75, 85, 88, 96, 107, 109, 129, 141, 159, 165, 174-175, 188
Photo Press: 2-3, 8-9. 32-33, 38-39, 46, 47, 55, 63, 64, 66, 80-81, 105, 106, 122, 147, 148, 155, 160-161, 190
Frank Spooner Pictures: 48
TRH Pictures: 13, 20-21, 35, 42, 44-45, 52, 53, 54, 56, 59, 69, 72, 77, 79, 82, 87, 91, 93, 95, 99, 100-101, 103, 110, 112,
   114, 116-117, 118, 126, 131, 132-133, 135, 137, 138-139, 150-151, 152, 156, 167, 168, 173, 177, 179, 183

ARTWORK CREDITS
Bob Garwood: 34, 41, 43, 53, 58, 62, 65, 67, 68, 70, 74, 76, 78, 84, 89, 94, 97, 102, 104, 108, 111, 119, 120, 121, 123,
   124, 125, 127, 128, 130, 140, 142, 143, 144, 145, 146, 149, 153, 157, 162, 163, 164, 166, 169, 170, 171, 172, 176, 177,
   178, 179, 180, 181, 182, 183, 184, 185, 186, 187 (both), 189
Chris West: 10, 11, 12, 13, 14, 15, 16, 17, 18, 19, 22, 23, 24, 25, 26, 27, 28, 29, 30, 31

Previous pages: A British Royal Marine sniper takes aim with his 7.62mm
Accuracy International PM rifle, one of the finest sniper rifles currently in
elite unit use.

CONTENTS

THE FIGHTING SKILLS IN ACTION

HANDS & SILENT WEAPONS

CHAPTER 1

THROWS & LOCKS

A lethal blend of martial arts techniques taken from many different styles is used by elite troops the world over to capture opponents, disarm attackers and escape from capture. Success in action depends on split-second timing, which can only be achieved through exhaustive practice.

The popular image of a special forces soldier is a man trained in all the martial arts, as well as in the use of a multitude of weapons. The reality is rather different. Western elite forces, for example, such as the British Special Air Service (SAS), US Green Berets, US Navy Sea-Air-Land (SEAL) teams and Belgian Para-Commandos, receive very little training in the martial arts. Though many members of each unit may be black belts in specific types of martial arts, this will be the result of proficiency in a hobby pursued in their spare time.

There are two main reasons why martial arts do not form an integral part of the training schedule of many special forces units. First, there is often not the time to fit martial arts training into busy schedules. Elite soldiers are expected to work in small teams on operations, often behind enemy lines and in hostile environments. To do so successfully requires each team member being proficient in a plethora of skills, such as demolitions, communications, medicine, survival, combat diving and parachuting, which in turn means he must spend many months on training courses. Second, the carrying of small arms has negated the effectiveness of many martial arts techniques. Unarmed combat and fighting with 'cold' weapons (staffs, knives, spears, clubs and the like) necessitates closing with the enemy – the last thing elite troops want to do.

Left: Spetsnaz trainees practice the deadly art of Sambo, the Russian combat martial art. Spetsnaz unarmed combat stresses lethal strikes.

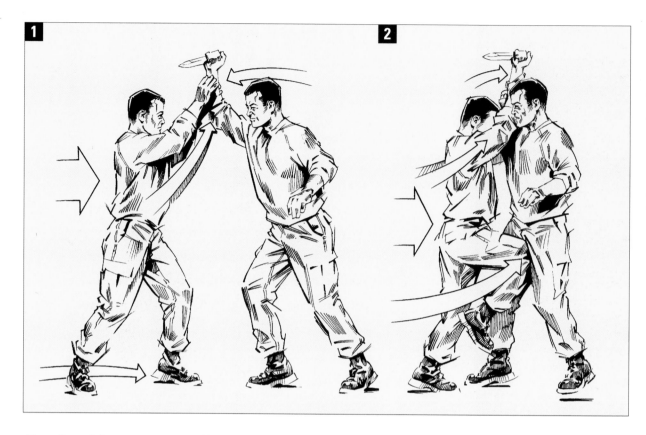

Above: A special forces technique for defeating an overhead stab. As soon as the attacking arm comes in the defender moves forward and grasps the wrist (1). Almost simultaneously, he delivers a knee strike to the attacker's groin (2).

Firearms allow teams to defeat enemy units without getting too close (the weapons skills of special forces soldiers often mean that an enemy attack can be broken up before opposition troops can get close enough to use their own weapons effectively). However, elite soldiers throughout the world do receive training in unarmed combat and silent killing techniques. But these have little to do with the highly organised and controlled martial arts techniques that are taught in *dojos* and training halls throughout the world, all under strict supervision with practitioners wearing the correct equipment and following each style's rules and regulations. Military unarmed combat has but one aim: to defeat the enemy by any means possible. The following is a quote from the training manual of Russia's massive intelligence agency, the KGB, but it could be from any special forces instruction booklet from around the world: 'This kind of combat [personal combat],

which may or may not use all kinds of personal weapons, develops a knowledge of defence and attack – of destroying a foe with a burst of automatic fire or a grenade; by bayonet, gun butt, knife or entrenching tool; with the fingers, the fist or knee; and by using incidental objects such as ropes, rocks and so on. Mastering the use of 'cold' weapons, useful objects, throws, choke holds (especially for capturing), or silent killing is done in actions at night, in woods, amid shattered buildings and so on.'

Compare the above quote with the origins of judo. Judo was created by Jigaro Kano in Japan in 1882 and emphasises throwing, sweeping and unbalancing techniques. It is essentially ju-jitsu with the punches and kicks taken out, to attain, in the words of Kano, 'the most efficient use of mental and physical energy'. Yet judo is still a fighting art, the holds and throws of which can be used to deadly effect by an elite soldier.

Judo was derived from ju-jitsu, and this ancient art provides many useful techniques for elite forces. The origins of ju-jitsu are lost in antiquity, but it was developed by numerous warrior, or Samurai, schools in Japan. Such schools specialised in archery, sword-fighting, tactics, horsemanship and so on, but unarmed combat techniques were also taught. They tended to be thought of as a last resort for the warrior who may have lost his weapon, or been taken by surprise with his sword sheathed. They were also useful if a high-ranking prisoner was to be taken alive for his ransom value.

The term ju-jitsu is often translated as 'the gentle art', but can also be thought of as 'the flexible art'. And it is this flexibility that gives it its usefulness to the modern soldier, as Ju-jitsu practitioners are taught techniques for a wide range of circumstances, from long-range kicks and strikes, to close-in grappling, throws, hand locks and attacks to the body's pressure points.

Ju-jitsu

Ju-jitsu incorporates combinations of blocks, strikes and throws to defeat an opponent, although it tends not to use many powerful blows to the head or body. This is probably a hangover from medieval times, when the enemy would be a soldier, often wearing protective armour and a helmet. The arms and legs would be the only vulnerable targets on such an opponent, hence the concentration on locks and various strikes to the joints.

A block or parry will be used to deflect a strike from an opponent, although the skilled ju-jitsu fighter will also move at the same time, initially to avoid the power of a blow, but also to position himself for the counter. This may be a strike to the neck, stomach or groin, followed by a throw, taking the opponent over his hips or legs and dumping him hard on the ground. This cannot be relied upon to neutralise a fit enemy soldier, especially if the combat is taking place on soft ground, so ju-jitsu often combines these throws with arm or wrist locks. For instance,

instead of carrying out a judo-style hip or shoulder throw, the special forces trooper may first twist his opponent's arms so that they are out straight, with the elbow downwards. He immediately twists into his enemy, placing the gripped arms over his shoulder, and bringing them down sharply to break or weaken the elbow joints. He can continue this motion into a hip throw, using the already damaged arm as the lever to take his opponent over his back. Once the throw is complete, the elite soldier will finish his victim with a strike or stamping kick to the neck, head or ribs, or with a further arm or wrist lock, leading to a joint break.

Ju-jitsu also covers chokes and strangles, although these are less effective against a fit soldier wearing heavy combat uniform and collar. And while the elite trooper will normally try and stay on his feet, should he be knocked to the ground or slip on unsure footing, ju-jitsu gives him techniques for defend-

Above: The third, and final, part of the movement. The defender yanks the attacker's knife hand down and twists the arm and wrist. The attacker, reeling with pain, drops the knife. Sounds easy? It requires countless hours of practice.

Above: A special forces defence against an underhand stab. In this scenario, the reflexes and timing of the defender have to be perfect. The defender steps inside and grasps the attacking arm (a cross-block can also be used).

nal power' which is a core belief of many Eastern philosophies. As a result some forms of aikido have become almost ballet-like, and virtually useless in combat situations. Others remain closer to traditional aiki-jitsu, and contain within them a number of techniques and approaches useful to the soldier.

Aikido is one of the least aggressive of martial arts, and is popular as a self-defence system, especially with people who do not wish to use the destructive techniques of ju-jitsu or karate. It also forms the basis of many police self-defence and restraint systems, especially taiho-jitsu, specially devised for the Tokyo police force.

Aikido

Aikido is concerned with controlling the force from an attacker, and using it against him to neutralise his attack. A skilled *aikidoka* will move in a seemingly effortless flowing manner to avoid an attack, taking the attacker's arm (for instance), leading him round in a circular movement, then dumping him back on the ground and pinning him with any one of a number of restraints. One difference between aikido and other martial arts is the former's emphasis on fighting multiple opponents at once, which is a much more realistic scenario than two fighters facing up to each other in a controlled one-on-one situation. There are many different wrist, arm, leg and neck joints used in aikido, which with minor adaptation can be useful weapons in an elite soldier's armoury. The art also contains a number of defence techniques against bladed weapons and clubs, and the movement skills of an aikido expert would be useful to any martial artist, no matter what system he or she fights in.

The key word is 'adapted'. All special forces soldiers receive instruction in unarmed combat techniques, whereas only certain elite units include pure martial arts instruction in their training routines. These units fall into one of three categories. First, there are the Eastern special forces units, such as the South Korean Special Forces,

ing himself or winning the fight from here. If a standing opponent tries to finish him off, the special forces soldier can kick to the side or front of his knees, which at best will immobilise his opponent, and at the least give him time to roll clear and get to his feet. More sophisticated ju-jitsu techniques include attacks to pressure points and nerve points, although these require a high level of skill and precision and are not often suitable for the military unarmed combat syllabus.

Another Japanese throwing art is aikido, which came from a variant of ju-jitsu known as aiki-jitsu, which was first recorded in the eleventh century. This was a complete fighting system which covered the use of sword and spear, as well as throws and restraints. In the 1930s, Morihei Ueshiba, a highly skilled student of aiki-jitsu, formed his own school, and began teaching an art which eventually became aikido. Ueshiba also saw aikido as a means of spiritual and personal development, especially concerned with the control and harnessing of *Ki*, the all-pervading 'inter-

Taiwanese Long-Range Reconnaissance Commandos and Thailand Special Forces. The selectors for these units put great emphasis on general education and martial arts training, as both are held to be strong indicators of 'spirit' or character. In South Korea, for example, there are strong ties between the martial arts establishment and the Special Forces.

The second category contains units such as Russia's Spetsnaz, which are trained to carry out sabotage, assassination and general de-stabilising missions in times of war, and in peacetime. The members of such units need to be very well versed in unarmed combat, able to kill opponents quickly and silently. Therefore, Spetsnaz soldiers are taught a combination of full-combat karate, judo and the Russian combat sport of sambo (*samooborona bez oruzhiye*).

Hostage-rescue units

The third category contains the members of the world's hostage-rescue and counter-terrorist teams. Rescuing hostages from armed terrorists requires anti-terrorist teams to get close to the hostage takers. Such scenarios require proficiency in close-quarter weapons drills, but may also demand unarmed skills. A silent approach during a rescue may require individual terrorists being 'taken out' silently with bare hands to avoid alerting other hostiles. What better than drawing upon the techniques of the martial arts? Units such as Germany's elite counter-terrorist *Grenzchutzgruppe* 9 (GSG 9) are thus fully trained in unarmed combat.

However, what the officers learn are not the traditional forms of the martial arts, because they are considered inappropriate for military and police close-quarter battle. Therefore, a range of techniques are taught from many martial arts styles. Aikido, for example, has excellent anti-knife techniques and wrist and arm blocks. Tae kwon do has many long-range kicks and strikes, while ju-jitsu combines pressure points and locks with throws. A blend of martial arts techniques is

Above: The second part of the movement. The defender delivers a kick to the attacker's groin – disabling him totally.

Left: US Army Rangers undergoing unarmed combat training, which forms an integral part of each recruit's curriculum.

Above: A Russian Spetsnaz technique for escaping when captured. When the hands are raised the guard holding the gun relaxes psychologically.

The first thing special forces recruits are taught is the anatomy of the human body. In this way they can learn how to kill with one blow, preferably silently. There are four main areas of the body that can be attacked.

The first area is the head and neck. Punches and blows delivered with the edge of the hand to the frontal lobe area produce bleeding and shock, while a blow with the fist to the back of the head can be fatal. The nose is a vulnerable point, with a strike with the side of the hand or a fist leading to fracturing, bleeding or death. An attack to the bridge of the nose can lead to fracturing and bleeding, and a punch or a kick to the temple can be fatal. While a fist or kick to the jaw will result in concussion, fracturing and pain, a blow with the edge of the hand to the carotid artery can result in death. A strike with the edge of the hand or a fist to the oesophagus will cause bleeding and even death, and the neck vertebrae can be broken with a fist or a blow with interlocked hands.

Joints and Collarbone

Joints and collarbone form the second area. The collarbone can be fractured with a blow with the side of the hand or the fist, while a punch or an elbow in the shoulder joint will result in extreme pain for the victim. The elbow or knee joint can also be attacked in the same way.

A punch or a kick to the solar plexus, the third area, will result in shock and great pain, while an attack to the liver will produce shock and pain. The kidneys can be attacked with the edge of the hand or a kick, and will result in pain and bleeding in the urinary tract. The groin is a very vulnerable area, which when attacked results in excruciating pain and shock.

The legs and feet comprise the fourth area. The knee joints and shins are very vulnerable to kicks or scraping, which can result in crippling pain, breaks, fractures and immobilisation.

The above techniques are often used when capturing opponents. The capture of a

ideal for hostage-rescue units. Defence against a terrorist with a gun requires the ability to sense the moment when the hostile is distracted. If the anti-terrorist operative decides to disarm the terrorist, the first strike with hands or feet will remove the weapon, while the second, usually a strike to a vital point like the throat, disables the target.

The techniques described in this and the next chapter are not an in-depth guide to various martial arts techniques. Rather, they are the holds, throws and strikes that are used by special forces members throughout the world. Charles Beckwith, the founder of Delta, the elite American counter-terrorist unit, also served with the British SAS. This unit, as mentioned above, does not train its men in the martial arts. However, it does instruct its members in killing techniques, and during his time with the SAS Beckwith learnt no less than 86 different ways to kill a human being.

prisoner is often used by special forces units as a way of collecting intelligence about the enemy. During World War II, for example, SAS and Special Boat Squadron (SBS) troops often abducted enemy sentries to gather information concerning German dispositions and plans.

The approach to the target is invariably from behind and in silence. One method of trapping a man is to approach from behind and twist the arm, followed by a strong blow to the elbow. Then a sharp blow with the hand to the shoulder takes the prisoner down for securing and escorting away.

A more ambitious method for capturing an enemy soldier, as used by Russia's Spetsnaz warriors, involves grabbing an enemy from behind by the shoulders, applying a kick to the back of the knee, holding the neck and then throwing the enemy to one side, and onto his back. It is then recommended that a sack or tunic be thrown over

the enemy's head and a choke hold applied. Strong pressure is used to stifle any shout, though not enough to suffocate the subject!

Capturing a seated enemy also requires an approach to the target from behind, pulling back the head with one hand, applying a choke hold with the other and then lifting the target from the chair.

Self-defence against Firearms

Hostage-rescue units, such as GSG 9 and the French *Groupement d'Intervention de la Gendarmerie Nationale* (GIGN), train their members to disarm armed terrorists with throws and holds. Speed and confidence are essential. If the distance to an opponent's weapon is less than one pace, for example, and he is armed with a handgun, then the best defence is to grab the hand holding the weapon and twist it inward, then step to the left and forward, turn to the right and then bend down to disarm the opponent.

Above: The Spetsnaz soldier strikes with one of his hands in a split-second (2), and then uses the other hand to take the weapon or knock it out of the guard's hand (3).

An opponent with a rifle at close range can be disarmed by grabbing the weapon and then either striking the opponent in the crotch or striking his throat or head with the knee or fist.

When confronted by an assailant armed with a bladed weapon such as a knife, the special forces soldier is taught to observe the way the knife is held. If the point is up and away from the thumb, for example, then a blow can be expected from below or from the side, towards the stomach, neck or side. However, if the point is down – away from the little finger – the blow will be overhand or backhand, towards the midriff or chest.

But the trick in defeating an opponent with a blade is to weigh up the situation and instinctively make the right moves. As the KGB's training manual states: 'the education of armed forces personnel has to put aside the usual, everyday methods of training: static teaching and lecturing, artificial situations and dummy weapons. Practical applications have shown that carrying out exercises on the street at any time of the year, wearing regular clothes and equipment, and using real "cold" weapons, disciplines the trainees, establishes a connection between personal defence and tactics, heightens interest and toughens the spirit.'

To defeat an overhand stab (right-handed), the defender moves his left foot forward and meets the descending knife arm of the assailant with his left forearm. Gripping the assailant's wrist or forearm with his right hand, the defender carries out an inward arm twist: turning to the right and stretching the attacker's knife arm as if it is being drawn towards the defender's right ear. Then, the assailant's arm is gripped under the defend-

Below: Basic elite throwing technique. The attacker grasps the defender (1) and then twists and bends to prepare for the throw (2).

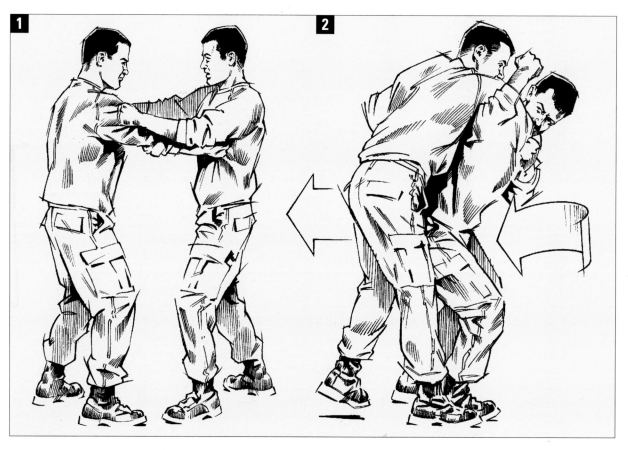

er's upper left arm, and then the defender's right hand is used to apply pain. The assailant's arm is then twisted behind his back (the knife can be expelled from his hand by using an inward twist of his hand and arm). The KGB's training manual then advises: 'To ensure complete success, a kick in the groin is essential.'

Underhand stabs can be defended against by using the forearm or two crossed forearms. A kick to the groin can then be applied. If the defender wishes to twist the attacker's weapon behind his back, then he has to advance his left foot to meet the attacker with his left arm, while at the same time bending forward slightly at the waist. The weapon arm is then grabbed with the defender's right hand and the attacker is kneed in the crotch. Alternatively, the attacker's weapon arm can be grasped and then he can be kicked in the crotch. This bends him forward, allowing the weapon hand to be twisted and the knife to be released. The attacker can then be kicked in the face.

SEAL Techniques

The US Navy's SEAL operatives are also instructed in all aspects of unarmed combat, as they frequently have to infiltrate hostile shorelines and kill enemy sentries. The SEAL training manual lays down the following procedure for defeating a backhand knife slash: 'Bend your knees and lower your body without ducking your head. At the same time, raise your right arm and block your opponent's thrust with your forearm or wrist. As soon as you block the blow, grasp your opponent's knife hand with your left hand. Apply pressure with your right wrist against his right wrist or forearm. Start to twist the knife hand to your left, and then reinforce your left hand hold with a similar hold with your right hand. Both your thumbs are now in the center of the back of his hand, and your fingers are around his palm. A twist to your left, or pressure that bends your opponent's hand forward and under against his wrist causes him to lose his weapon and, in

many cases, to suffer a broken or dislocated wrist at the very least.'

If the enemy has a machete, axe or entrenching tool, the attack will most likely be a swinging, circular motion, probably aimed at the head, neck or upper body. In this case the defender needs to move aggressively into this attack, blocking the swinging arm before it has a chance to build up momentum. This block, if carried out with enough force, will temporarily break the attacker's balance, leaving him vulnerable to a throw or lock. A similar technique is used if the attacker has a club of some sort.

The above techniques for defeating an attack from a bladed weapon are straightforward enough, though it must be remembered

Above: The attacker, having lifted the defender's armpit with one arm, then throws his opponent over his shoulders so he lands on his head.

that attacks with a knife are invariably multiple and frenzied, not the single, telegraphed attack. A successful defence demands a high level of skill, and even a martial arts master can expect to be cut at least during a knife attack. Speed and accuracy are essential when dealing with a knife-wielding attacker.

Elite troops run the risk of being captured on operations, especially during missions behind enemy lines. But capture may not necessarily mean the end of the mission. Even the act of surrendering can be turned to advantage. Russian Spetsnaz troops are taught how to deal with an armed guard holding a pistol. Immediately after the 'hands up' order has been given, the Spetsnaz warrior lifts his arms as ordered. Psychologically the guard relaxes, feeling he has the captive at his mercy. However, in a flash, the Spetsnaz soldier strikes with one of his hands and grabs the weapon arm, pushing it to one side. The free hand is then used to knock the

Below: A hip throw. The thrower has advanced his right foot towards his opponent's right foot, then made a body turn and placed his right arm around his opponent's waist. He then throws his opponent over his hip.

pistol out of the guard's hand or to take it. This move requires expert timing.

A guard holding a levelled rifle can be disarmed by moving forward to the right, turning to the left, grabbing the weapon with the left hand and then pushing it away. The guard is then hit in the face or throat with the right hand, while the Spetsnaz soldier's right foot is used to deliver a kick in the bend of the guard's knee.

Even a guard pointing a weapon at the back of a special forces soldier can be defeated. By turning round to the right and seizing and bending the guard's weapon hand arm outward or inward, it is possible to disarm him. However, in all these instances the words of the Spetsnaz unarmed combat manual are very pertinent: 'You have to get it [the weapon] as quickly as possible'.

Throws

The throws learned by elite troops are very similar to those practised by martial arts specialists, though adapted for military purposes. The most common taught to elite troops are the backward throw, the forward throw over the shoulder and the throw by sweeping an opponent's legs from under him. The instructors stress that the throws must be successful, 'even at the expense of a beautiful, technical flawless performance'.

The forward throw over the shoulder is used against an attack from behind or holds on the neck. With one hand lifting the opponent's armpit, the throw is performed with knees flexed and the enemy is thrown over the shoulders to land on his head.

The backward throw involves a throw across the thigh, with a simultaneous elbow to the face or fingers in the eyes or nostrils. Similarly, a tripping throw with an attack to the crotch or throat is very effective.

Throws that involve grabbing an opponent's legs are preceded by blows in order to stun an opponent. Without this prior attack this kind of throw would be inviting serious injury or even death against an alert and strong opponent.

Left: Russian Spetsnaz soldiers learning unarmed combat, in this case how to deal with an opponent armed with a rifle fitted with a bayonet.

Below: Sweeping an opponent's legs. The defender first sweeps his opponent's legs together (1), lifts him and throws him to the ground (2).

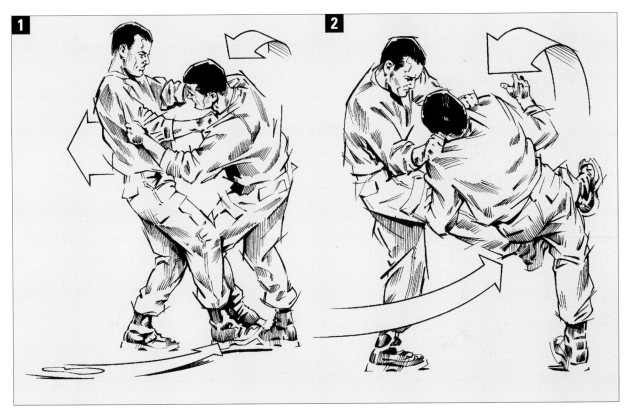

CHAPTER 2

STRIKES & BLOWS

Elite soldiers are trained to use their hands, feet, elbows, knees and head to deadly effect in combat, but their techniques for doing so are very different from the ritualistic martial arts practised throughout the world. Military strikes and blows stress violence of action coupled with minimum force.

M any elite forces teach their members elements of karate, kung fu and tae kwon do. Turning hands and feet into deadly weapons is obviously a way of increasing the overall effectiveness of a single special forces soldier, allowing him to become a human force multiplier, capable of killing even when he has no weapons.

The origins of karate are open to argument, but most sources agree that it was developed on Okinawa. Under Japanese occupation for most of their history, the Okinawans developed their art as an unarmed combat system, as they were forbidden from carrying weapons. They took influences from Chinese martial arts, and a multitude of styles evolved, ranging from fluid, almost ju-jitsu-like styles to the more rigid, 'power-based' styles. What weapons are taught have been derived from modified farming implements, such as the three-pronged *sai* (originally a short pitchfork used to lift hay-bales), the *tonfa* (side-handled grinding sticks), which is the model for modern side-handled law-enforcement batons, and the *nanchuk*, (rice flail), which is two heavy sticks linked by a short length of chain. Karate (meaning 'open hand') is probably the most popular sport and recreational martial art in the world, and many of its striking and blocking techniques are applicable to the combat soldier, especially those who operate behind the lines.

Left: Potential recruits to Britain's Parachute Regiment during 'milling': a minute of violence which reveals if they are made of the 'right stuff'.

Above: A typical special forces fighting stance. The pose is relaxed, the fists in front of the chest, legs bent at the knees and leading leg forward.

stant practice and a high level of skill to perform well in a combat situation, especially if the ground surface is less than perfect. They are unlikely to be seen in use apart from by those special forces units (such as the Korean Special Forces) that specialise in this form of unarmed combat

Chinese Martial Arts

There are a multitude of Chinese martial arts referred to under the umbrella term of kung fu. Many take their name and inspiration from observing the animal world, such as 'crane-style' kung fu, which incorporates fast, high-jabbing attacks with hands and feet, aimed at vulnerable pressure points. Wing chun specialises in close-range combat and has many useful striking and grappling techniques for the soldier. Chinese systems tend to use a different method of striking to Japanese and Korean methods, where the muscles of the striking arm or leg remain relaxed until just before impact, when they are tensed in a sudden spasm. This method is said to allow a faster strike, although it does demand a high level of training. In practice, both this method and the 'harder' striking styles of karate and tae kwon do seem to have the same end effect.

The origins and subtle differences in style and technique are of no importance to elite units. What is important is the blows with hands and feet that the different styles utilise. As with throws and holds, the techniques are adapted to suit elite unit requirements. After all, complex movements that take several seconds are of little use when the same result – the death or disabling of an opponent – can be achieved with a one-second movement.

Students are taught to make use of all the body's weapons, not just the hands and feet, when attacking an opponent. These weapons are many and varied.

The head is excellent for butting from the right, left, front or rear with the front, corner or rear of the head. The crown of the head can also be used to make an upward attack.

Tae kwon do originated in Korea, and is a close relative of karate. Korean martial arts have a long and distinguished history, but the name tae kwon do was not actually adopted until the 1950s, when the art was systematised by Korean martial artists and the military. It absorbed elements and techniques from many Korean, Japanese and Chinese arts, but is characterised by its repertoire of spectacular high kicks, often combined with a leaping and spinning action. Martial artists constantly argue about the real effectiveness of such techniques, but there is no denying that they require con-

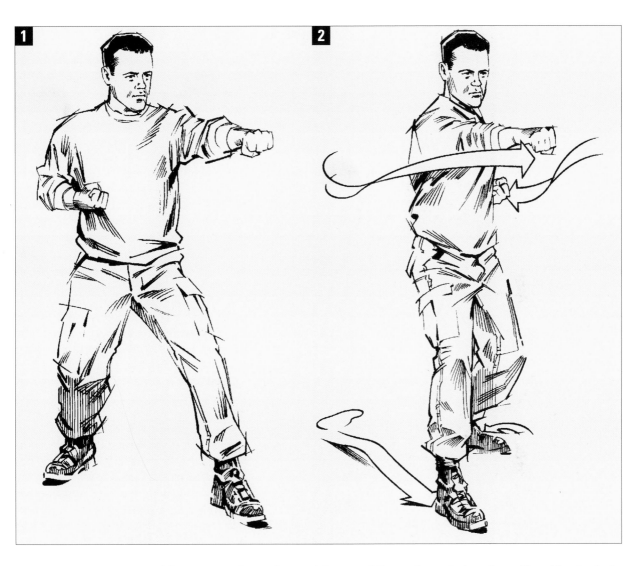

The elbows are very good from any angle during a close-quarter engagement, while the hands can be used for punching in any direction, also for gouging and jabbing with the fingers. The knees can be used to thrust upward into the groin, body or head of an opponent, and the feet can be used to attack any part of an opponent's anatomy. They are particularly effective for attacking the lower regions of the body: groin, knees and shins.

The Fist

One of the first things a martial arts student learns is how to make a fist. The same is true of special forces soldiers. The technique is simple enough: the hand is opened out fully, then the fingers are curled down so they touch the pad of flesh running along the top of the palm. After this the fingers are folded forward from the knuckles, and then the fist is closed by folding the thumb across the index and middle fingers (the target is usually hit with the index and middle finger knuckles only).

Delivery of the punch is all-important. Elite units teach their recruits to adopt a stance with the feet shoulder-width apart, then (for a right-handed punch) to move the

Above: The standard punch. In the first part of the movement (1), the left leg is extended and the right fist tucked back. The attacker quickly steps forward with his right foot, pulls back his left arm and punches with his right fist (2).

left foot forward a pace and a half, bend the left knee and straighten the right knee, ensure both hips face the front, then extend the left arm forward and straighten the elbow. The right fist is held palm up just above the waist. The student then moves forward with the right foot and snaps out a punch with the right fist. This is called the lunge punch.

The jab begins with a so-called 'walking stance'. This is where one foot leads the other by a pace and the fists are held in a guard position in front of the body, usually at the height of the chest or the head. To make a jab with the left fist requires sliding the left foot forward half a pace, bending both knees slightly to lower the centre of gravity, then pulling the right fist back hard to the chest and using this action to help thrust out a sharp punch with the left.

Below: Elbows can be more powerful than hands if used correctly. This side elbow into an attacker's face will knock him to the ground.

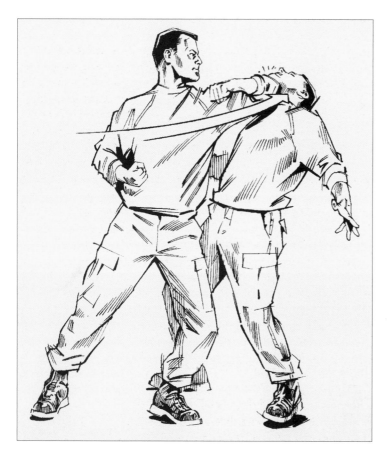

Learning to punch correctly, though, is only one part of the equation. Hitting the right spot is the other. Strikes to the body should be penetrative – striking the central nervous system – and in the case of to the head, accurate. Attacking the head above an opponent's eye line, for example, is futile. For one thing, on the battlefield he is likely to have a steel helmet on, but even if he didn't the cranium is strongly constructed to protect the brain, and a strike there would have little effect. Similarly, an attack to the nose can be borne by an opponent and should be discounted.

It is different with regard to the eyes and jaw, however. Any successful attack against the eyes will incapacitate an opponent. A finger in an eye can produce a collapsed eyeball, lacerated eyelid or even the eyeball being pushed out of its socket. An impact to the jaw, if struck correctly, will render an opponent unconscious.

A successful strike to the throat can cause contusions, partial and complete paralysis of the victim, even death. However, as elsewhere, the key word here is 'successful'.

The torso is large and would seem to beckon as a target. However, opposition soldiers will usually be wearing webbing, baggy smocks and maybe even body armour, which will all defeat the blow.

Elbows

Elbows are very useful weapons in close-quarter combat; because they are close to the body they can be, if used correctly, more powerful than the hands. On the debit side, though, they can lack the 'feel' and accuracy of the hands.

The elbows can be used for downward strikes, side strikes and reverse strikes.

With downward strikes the left or right arm is lifted up high with the palm of the hand facing towards the body. It is then pulled down quickly, driving the point of the elbow into an opponent's spine, neck or rib cage. This is a particularly effective strike, which is taught to all elite troops.

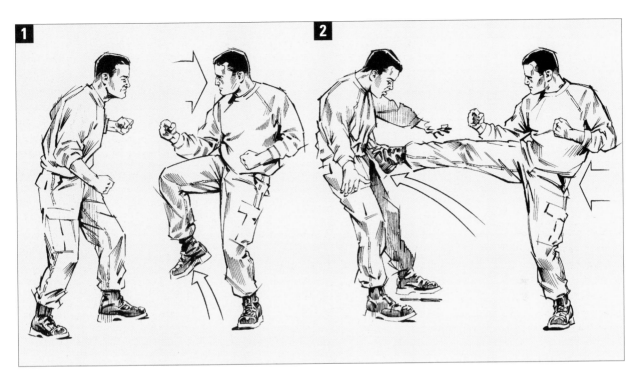

Side strikes are very useful against an opponent attacking from the side. The right or left arm is brought across the front of the chest, palm inwards, as far as it will go. It is then thrust back along the same direction, crashing the point of the elbow into the attacker's face, throat or solar plexus.

Reverse strikes are useful against an attacker behind you. The right or left arm is stretched out in front, while the head is turned to look at the target. The arm is then quickly retracted from its outstretched position and shot back, aiming the point of the elbow at the attacker, and at the same time stepping back with the leg that corresponds to the attacking elbow to add more weight, and thus power, to the attack.

Kicks

The feet are also powerful attacking tools, though harder to master than the hands. Traditional martial arts such as karate teach students to strike with the ball or side of the feet so as to maximise the effect and not damage the toes. Elite troops wearing boots

obviously do not need to worry so much about this, but they do have to master the technique of kicking correctly if they are to use their feet in combat.

A typical front kick would be the one taught in tae kwon do. To kick with the right foot, the knees are slightly bent with the left foot forward. The right leg is brought forward and up so it passes close by the left knee. The right knee is then lifted higher than the target and then dropped as the lower leg is snapped out to make contact.

The side kick is extremely powerful, though it requires a high degree of skill to execute successfully. When attacking to the side, the knee of the attacking leg is lifted upwards and the foot thrust sideways at the target. At the same time, the student pivots on his supporting leg so that the foot of the supporting leg is pointing in the opposite direction from the target.

The roundhouse kick requires even more skill, but is excellent for attacking the ribs, kidneys, lower abdomen, groin, thighs, knees and shins. The trick is to lift the knee of the

Above: A military style front kick. From a fighting stance, the attacker snaps his right lower leg forward and up at the knee (1). He then snaps the lower part of the leg to strike the enemy's stomach or groin area.

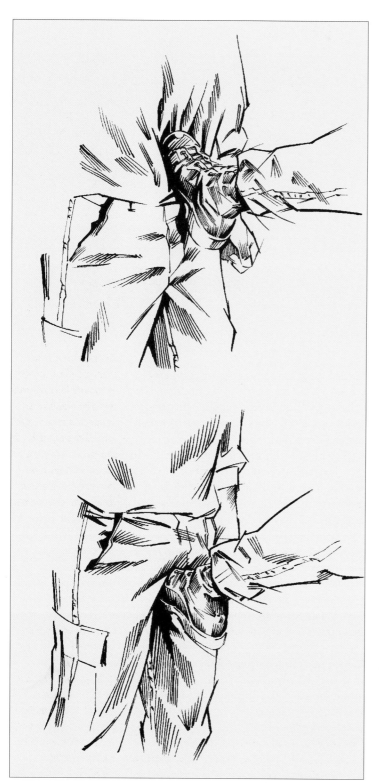

attacking leg high and to the side, to throw the lower leg around and into the target by pivoting on the supporting leg and thrusting the hips behind the kick.

The back kick is another strong technique, excellent when striking with the heel to attack the groin, solar plexus, ribs, thighs and knees. To use the right leg requires leading with the left leg. The right leg is lifted up towards the left and its in-step wrapped tightly around the left leg's calf. The student turns his head to keep sight of the target at all times, then thrusts the heel of his right foot into the target.

Kicks from a Lying Position

It is an important part of the conditioning of elite soldiers that their instructors emphasise the importance of never giving up. With this in mind, a number of techniques have been developed for launching kicks while lying on the ground and under attack. If the defender falls to the ground, then it is imperative for him to get into a good defensive position because the attacker will immediately go for the kill. This means using the knees and elbows to act as cover for the groin, body and

head. From such a position it is possible to hook one foot behind the attacker's advancing foot to give leverage and then lash out with the other to strike his shin. Before the attacker can recover, it is possible to lash out at his groin or knees.

The aim is to get up as quickly as possible, for the longer you are on the ground the less your chance of ever getting up again. An attacker attempting punches can be defeated with parries, which gives the defender time to get up.

Putting Theory into Practice

Elite forces train by incorporating the above-mentioned punches and kicks in a variety of scenarios: escaping and fighting off attacks from behind, escaping and fighting in single combat, and giving assistance to an escape attempt. The Spetsnaz training manual is very succinct when it comes to using strikes: 'In escaping being grabbed, you should, above all, utilise the most vulnerable points of an enemy's body: the head, the ears, the throat, the sex organs and so on. If an enemy gets you down on the ground, you have to continue the struggle by using your knee, by

choking, biting, gouging and kicking.' Successful strikes rely on lightning speed, accuracy and aggression. For example, to escape from a frontal choke hold special forces unarmed trainers recommend grabbing an opponent's crotch. This is done in a forceful way, twisting back and forth and trying to pull the opponent towards you.

To escape from restraints and holds, students are taught to use their index and middle fingers to jab the eyes, and to use hands, arms and elbows to deliver blows. However, one of the body's most offensive weapons is the head.

The Head

As mentioned above, strikes to an opponent's head must be made below the eye line (and the attacker must use the area above the eye line of his head to deliver a strike). The head may be used for an attack in five different ways: with the left corner of the forehead, with the right corner of the forehead, with the centre of the forehead, with the crown of the head, and with the back of the head.

Success when using the head butt relies on two things: the whiplash effect as the

Above: The side kick involves the attacker lifting his leg upwards and pivoting on the supported leg (1). The heel is then thrust into the target. The kick to the rear (3) involves the attacker observing the target at all times.

Opposite page: If an opponent is wearing civilian clothes or light military attire, a kick to the stomach is effective (top). If the stomach is protected, a kick to the groin is recommended (bottom).

Above: Elite soldiers are trained to fight from the ground. A blow to an attacker's shin is very effective for stopping his assault, which buys the defender time.

Right: Spetsnaz kicking techniques. A club-wielding attacker's blow is blocked with the forearm and then he is disabled with a front kick.

attacker thrusts his body forward before the head, thereby forcing the head to follow and thus creating the whiplash effect, and forward-moving body weight, which adds to the overall attack.

Attacking with the left and right corners of the head involves using the corners of the forehead to crash into the right, left or front of an opponent's nose, face or jaw. The attack can be aided if the attacker is gripping the opponent's clothing, for he can be pulled towards the head butt.

When attacking with the centre of the head, the attacker launches his body forward, followed by the front of his head, whiplashing it into the opponent's eyes, nose or jaw. Great care must be taken not to hit an opponent's teeth with the forehead. Even though this will undoubtedly knock them all out, the teeth are a potential danger to the attacker.

Attacking with the crown of the head is a method that is generally used when grappling with an opponent. Ideally the attacker's forehead should be in the region of the opponent's chest. From this position the forehead is thrust upwards into an opponent's chin with the front crown of the head.

Attacking with the back of the head can be just as effective. This is used when an opponent is standing directly behind or is executing a rear bear-hug. If the enemy is standing behind, the attacker throws his body backwards followed by his head, thus whiplashing the back of the skull into his face. If the enemy is executing a bear-hug he has effectively immobilised the body. However, the head can still be used. It is bent forward slightly and then thrown backwards as quick-

ly as possible to smash the back of the skull into the enemy's face.

The head butt itself is rarely used on its own. North and South Korean Special Forces, along with their Spetsnaz counterparts, are taught to combine blows and blocks for maximum effect. For example, when dealing with an enemy who is wielding a club or similar object, the defender blocks the blow with his forearm and uses the fingers on his other hand to jab at the eyes. Or, after the block, the defender steps forward and head butts the attacker in his face. This drops his head, after which a hard blow is delivered to the attacker's crotch. This will without doubt drop him to the floor.

Below: A roundhouse knee strike. When attacked, the defender moves his right foot slightly back (1), then lifts his right knee and smashes it into the attacker (2).

Training for unarmed combat is all very well, but many real situations are not so clear cut. In World War II, British Commando training emphasised close-range fighting in its entirety; volunteers would be trained in environments where hands, feet, knives, improvised weapons and firearms were simultaneously used. The aim was to condition the mind to fight to win in any situation, and prepare the soldiers to be adaptable and able to deal with the unexpected at all times. If a soldier was conditioned to think that 'if we're on the ranges, we're doing pistol shooting' and 'if we're in the gym, it's unarmed combat', then he would not be properly prepared for the chaos and pressure of a real combat situation.

Below: A simple finger jab can, at worst, knock an eyeball out of its socket.

Britain's SAS follows similar principles today in its CQB (Close-Quarters Battle) training. This has a strong internal security and undercover element, and is intended to train its troopers to fight and win under any circumstances. The key is acting correctly under pressure to any level of threat, emphasising rapid, instinctive decision-making and action. An undercover soldier may have to face up to threats ranging from a simple pub brawl, an unarmed attempt to attack or capture him, or a deadly attack with firearms or blades. In many of these situations, drawing a pistol and starting to shoot may be unjustifiable, illegal and would completely compromise his mission.

The SAS trooper is taught to deal with confused situations with multiple attackers, and where there may be confused or terrified bystanders milling about. For instance, he may have to shoulder civilians out of the way or to the ground, while at the same time engage an armed terrorist with a firearm. He is taught how to combine fast, deadly accurate pistol and submachine-gun fire with tactical movement and a range of unarmed techniques. Tactics play an important part, especially how to fight in enclosed spaces such as alleyways, bars, lifts and hallways. Vehicles are also incorporated into the syllabus, including fast driving, how to fire from them, and how to leave or enter them in a high-threat environment.

Speed and Aggression

The martial arts elements of the course are simple and brutal, emphasising absolute confidence and aggression, and speedy resolution of the action. Simple techniques have a better chance of working when under pressure, especially those which do not require a specific set of circumstances to work. Many *dojo* techniques, while effective in training, require absolute precision, with the operator's feet or hands exactly placed, and with the opponent in exactly the right position. If these circumstances aren't met, the technique fails completely. Real combat tech-

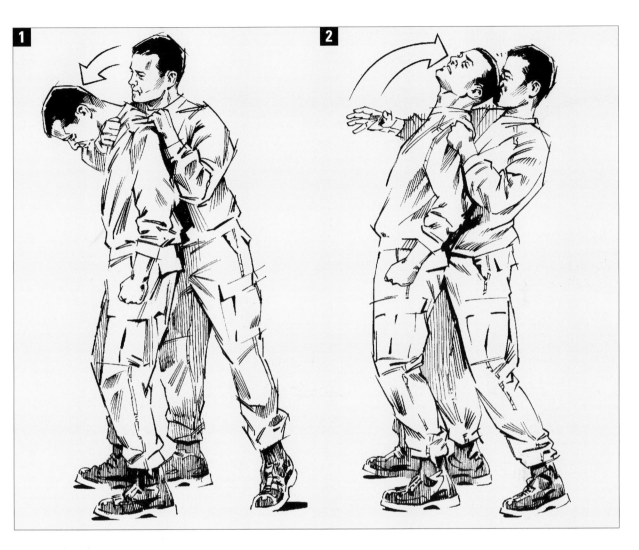

niques need to be rough and ready, and able to work if the enemy is not exactly where you need him to be, or if you are not in the correct fighting stance, or if you miss the exact target spot. As SAS Sergeant Andy McNab, whose exploits during the 1991 Gulf War became famous in his book *Bravo Two Zero*, wrote: 'It would be arms and legs everywhere, head butts, biting and gouging.'

McNab gives another reason for such 'basic' techniques, highly relevant to undercover operators: 'If we got cornered in Northern Ireland and did a Bruce Lee, they were going to say, "He knew what he was doing. It looked too clear and precise –

there's something wrong". But if it just looked like a good old scrap with ears torn and noses bitten off, they'd think it was a run-of-the-mill street fight and nothing to do with the security forces.'

McNab might also have mentioned another quality required in unarmed combat: the will to kill. Some might say that in the white heat of combat soldiers are running on adrenalin, so conscious will does not matter. But elite soldiers are trained to remain cool and keep the brain working under great stress. Therefore, the will to kill with hands and feet has to be present, allied to high skill and cold intent.

Above: The head can be a fearsome weapon. Even if held in a choke hold, an elite soldier can bring his head forward (1), and then throw it back to execute a reverse head butt (2).

CHAPTER 3

EDGED
WEAPONS

Knives and bayonets are very important implements to elite soldiers, but they are used more for the more mundane field activities that the close-quarter killing of popular imagination. Nevertheless, the right choice of blade is still very important for the individual on special forces missions.

t is a popular misconception that elite troops on covert missions behind enemy lines frequently kill their opponents with a knife or bayonet. Though on occasion special forces soldiers will have to call on their skills with an edged weapon, the reality is that knives and bayonets are usually used as a last resort.

Not that training in the use of edged weapons is not given to elite soldiers, far from it. The training manual of the US Navy's SEALs, for example, is extremely graphic about how to deal with enemy sentries during an inland raid: 'If possible, get to within six feet of a sentry before attacking him.' The manual then recommends several ways of despatching the sentry with edged weapons. If using a knife, it 'is an effective weapon when used on a victim's kidneys or throat'. If using an entrenching tool, 'keep the cutting edge of entrenching tools extremely sharp. They are good silent weapons and can be used in lieu of a machete. From the rear, give a powerful direct blow to small of the back, kidney or (if the sentry is not wearing a helmet) the base of the skull.'

Similarly, Russian Spetsnaz troops are given precise instruction on the use of the knife: 'Steal up behind the enemy or stalk him down a path. Put your left hand over his mouth and cut his throat with the knife in your hand ... Stabbing the throat is learned for security's sake, in the event that a targeted enemy turns towards

Left: The bayonet, a weapon whose impact in battle has been more psychological than physical. However, all soldiers are trained in its use.

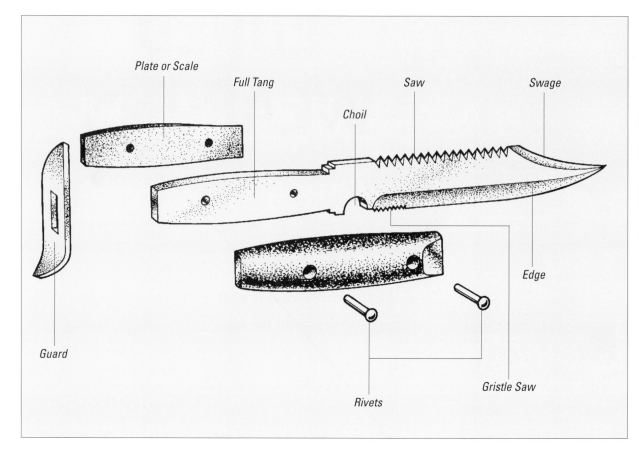

Plate or Scale

Full Tang

Saw

Swage

Choil

Edge

Guard

Gristle Saw

Rivets

Above: A good special forces knife has a full tang, generous guard and a blade with two different edges.

the direction of the attack. Right after a stab, you have to grapple with the enemy and get him down on the ground, shut his mouth, and – most important – keep him from firing his weapon.' Hair-raising stuff indeed!

But learning to wield a knife correctly takes hundreds of hours of practice. The British SAS's Training Wing, for example, has determined that it takes 2400 repetitions of a movement, combined with realistic exercises to make it into an instinctive drill, to fully train one of its soldiers so he is able to 'take out' an enemy soldier silently. But elite forces have found that there is another problem with regard to teaching its men to slit an opponent's throat. To kill a man with an edged weapon up close and in 'cold blood' not only takes skill, it also requires an emotional detachment. Elite forces do not recruit killers, they enlist personnel who can kill as

and when professionally necessary. In addition, only intense training can foster this emotional detachment, but time is at a premium when it comes to training elite troops, and often there is little left to teach knife skills. There are exceptions, of course, and these are discussed below.

The Knife

Notwithstanding the above, the knife is an extremely important part of the equipment of an elite soldier. In the field it is useful for digging holes, opening tins and cutting wood for fires. This goes for bayonets, too. For hostage-rescue specialists, a knife serves a similar purpose to a diver's knife: useful for cutting free of entanglements and the like. Killing comes way down the list. A typical military knife is the Buck M9 field knife which entered service with the US Army in

1996 as its standard-issue bayonet. It has a 'zone heat-treated' 180mm (7in) forged-steel blade. The blade itself has a saw-toothed back edge that will cut through rope, ice (for cutting blocks for shelters in polar regions), wood and even aircraft fuselage metal. In addition, when it is coupled with a stud on the rugged plastic sheath, it becomes a wire cutter. The US Navy's elite SEAL teams normally carry a simple stainless steel knife, which is worn on a web belt or strapped to the diver's leg.

The choice of metal is important to how a knife performs in combat. There are two choices of metal when it comes to knives: stainless steel or carbon steel. Generally speaking, carbon steel rusts unless cared for, whereas stainless steel will not. Carbon steel allows the user to achieve a keener edge, more so than stainless steel, but stainless steel should hold its edge longer. That said, it is harder to sharpen than carbon steel. Stainless steel is often regarded as the best

choice (though it is usually blended with other metals, such as vanadium, molybdenum and chromium, which all change its properties). Another potential problem is the knife's temper. If a knife is under-tempered it will be strong but won't take an edge, whereas if it is over-tempered it could shatter in use. A full tang (the extension of the blade which fits into the handle) will substantially improve the weapon overall, as it makes the knife considerably stronger.

Regardless of the exact model used, all special forces knives have similar characteristics. They all have a blade guard, which provides protection for the hand, plus a finger spot, which the little finger wraps around when holding the weapon for defence. This finger spot or groove is at the base of the blade itself, but it is smooth so as not to cut the hand. The handle itself is hard so it can be used for striking. The blade is usually double-edged, though the back blade, like that on the above-mentioned Buck knife,

Left: A selection of military knives. The knife is useful to a soldier because of its attributes as a tool and for use in survival situations. Its value as a killing implement comes well down the list.

Above: The machete, excellent for cutting wood and foliage but rather limited as a weapon, being clumsy having only one cutting edge.

is often serrated and can be used as a saw. The two blades mean the knife can be used for cutting and slashing forwards and backwards. Maintaining the blade's sharpness is imperative, and it is normal for troops to carry a small stone for such a purpose. Sharpening a blade involves maintaining an even pressure across the full width of the edge of the blade (elite troops spend a great deal of time sharpening their knives – a blunt knife is not just an inefficient tool, it is also a dangerous liability to its owner).

Knife Grips

The knife's grip is extremely important as it determines whether the user will have exact and secure control of the blade. If a grip is too large, for example, it is difficult to hold onto; if too short the user may have difficulty in holding the knife correctly – potentially lethal in a close-quarter combat situation. As a general rule special forces soldiers go for a grip that is slightly too big, because it is less tiring to use and makes the knife easier to hold when wearing gloves.

As a weapon, the entrenching tool does not, in general, feature highly in the

armoury of elite forces. Nevertheless, there is one unit that trains in the use of the entrenching tool and has used it to devastating effect on occasion: Russia's Spetsnaz. The use of the entrenching tool as an offensive arm in Russian service stretches back to World War II, or the Great Patriotic War as it is known in the countries of the former Soviet Union. The nature of the fighting on the Eastern Front in 1941-45, particularly in winter, meant there was significant close-quarter action. German and Russian troops would close with each other and would often engage in hand-to-hand fighting. This involved the sharpened edges of entrenching tools, as well as knives and bayonets. Over 50 years later, the KGB's training manual lists the entrenching tool as an effective weapon: 'The use of an entrenching tool as a means of defence is written about extensively in military literature. Blows with it are delivered overhand, from the side, as slashes to the face, and so on.'

Using the entrenching tool requires great speed and accuracy to land blows to the head, neck and shoulders. The entrenching tool needs to be swung with great force for maximum effectiveness, which means it is often wielded two-handed, much the same as a medieval battle axe.

Spetsnaz used bladed weapons to great effect during the war in Afghanistan during the 1980s. Spetsnaz units often undertook convoy protection duties against *Mujahedeen* forces, usually being dropped by helicopter on the crests of hills ahead of the convoy. Such operations involved expertise in mountain fighting techniques and close-quarter combat. They were carried out during the 1985 Kunar and Paktia offensives and the 1987-88 relief of the city of Khost. The Spetsnaz units invariably moved at night against *Mujahedeen* positions, being dropped on one mountain crest and then making a covert approach to seize an enemy held post. This usually involved climbing hundreds of metres and then rushing the enemy with bayonets and entrenching tools. These tactics were effective, and one *Mujahedeen* leader, Jalat Khan, described the Spetsnaz troops as being able to 'kill very well'.

Machetes

The machete is a useful tool for jungle operations, having a long blade and being significantly heavier than a knife. However, as a tool for close-quarter killing it leaves a lot to be desired. For one thing, it is unwieldy when compared to the knife, and is only designed to be used with a slashing movement. For thrusting it is useless. One counter-terrorist unit that reportedly uses the machete as a weapon is Brazil's 1st Special Forces Battalion Counter-Terrorist Detachment. Brazil's extensive area of jungle has necessitated members of the unit becoming experts in jungle warfare techniques, especially stalking targets in the often impassable tropical forests. Members of the unit have lived and trained with several Amazon tribes, and are again reportedly expert at killing with the knife and machete.

But probably the most famous machete weapon in military use is the kukri, the curved knife of the Gurkhas. This has a broad blade, which is curved at a sharp angle halfway along its length. While it has a sharp point, it is normally used as a chopping weapon, able to inflict fearsome damage in the correct hands. But the true value of the kukri is probably as a weapon against enemy morale – the reputation of the Gurkhas is such that the sight of a small Nepalese soldier with a broad grin and this ferocious knife is enough to strike terror into almost any enemy. As with the bayonet, its impact is more psychological than physical.

Left: The Gurkha kukri. Opinion is divided over what is more frightening, the weapon itself or the Gurkha wielding it.

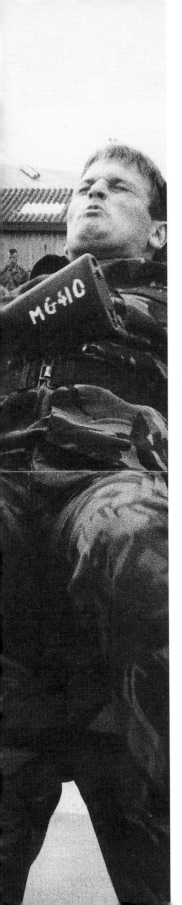

CHAPTER 4

IMPROVISED WEAPONS

Simple pieces of wood can be used by elite troops to fashion clubs or make bows to strike at enemy soldiers, and such innocuous items such as ordinary socks filled with sand can be turned into deadly instruments. All it takes is the right materials and a little imagination.

All special forces soldiers are taught the art of combat survival. This enables them to live off the land in an emergency, when their food supplies have become exhausted. The US Green Berets, for example, include in their five-week Q Course Phase I survival techniques, and these skills are tested in a 12-night exercise in the wild at the end of the course. Combat survival involves being able to fashion weapons from locally available materials in order to hunt prey, as well as the skill to lay traps to catch wild animals for food.

These same skills can be used to make improvised weapons to kill human beings, and this chapter will examine some of them. One of the most effective homemade weapons is the staff, which can be easily fashioned from materials to hand. The staff is a simple piece of straight wood that is approximately 1m (3ft) in length. In the hands of police units it is a common enough sight, and is used all over the world for crowd control. In the hands of special forces it is used differently, but the weapon is still essentially the same. The staff is carried by North Korean special forces during their raids across the border into South Korea, and can be used with deadly effect. A staff can be easily fashioned from a branch cut from a tree; in the hands of an elite soldier it becomes a ferocious weapon.

Left: A British Royal Marine Commando demonstrates how an M16 assault rifle can be used as an improvised club to kill opponents.

Holding the staff the correct way is imperative for maximum effectiveness. It is not held in the middle, but rather by grasping the shaft approximately 150mm (6in) from one end. It is held as one would hold a tennis racquet: with all four fingers wrapped around it and the thumb riding along the top or wrapped around the fingers.

As well as being used as an offensive weapon, the staff can be used to block an opponent's attack in a number of ways. The 'X' block involves snapping the hands down in front of the groin with both arms crossing each other in front of the body, while one hand is holding the staff. The open groin block entails snapping the staff to block the groin as above, only this time the arms are not crossed. The two-handed side block involves snapping the staff across the body and blocking the chest area (the staff is held vertically in front of the body). The high block, also called rising block, raises the staff to head height, where it is held horizontally with two hands ready to receive a blow.

Attacking with the Staff

It is as an offensive tool, though, that the staff shows its true worth, becoming in the hands of a trained specialist an awesome weapon. The staff can be used either to smash or thrust. It can be thrust into the eyes and throat, and smashed across the side of the face, collarbone, back of the head or spine, ribs, up into the groin, kneecap, between the eyes or to the throat.

Often a simple block can stop a strike with a staff, so many elite troops have learnt techniques for overcoming this. For, example, if an overhead strike to the head of an enemy is met with a rising block, a simple flip of the wrist will cause the block to fall short and allows the staff to hit its target.

Similarly, if a side swing is blocked with the forearm, the wrist can be flipped out and extended to ensure the staff still hits the head (the head will be avoided as a target if an opponent is wearing a steel helmet, which will defeat a blow).

As well as being a superb attacking weapon, the staff can be a powerful defensive aid aside from the blocking techniques mentioned above. Defensive moves revolve around smashing the staff onto an enemy's striking arm or leg. For example, when holding the staff with the right hand, an elite soldier can wait for an opponent to hit out with a fist or blade. When he does, the staff is used to smash the opponent's elbow. The staff is then driven into the opponent's kidneys, which will cause him to collapse to the ground, where he is finished off with a staff attack to his neck.

Potential grabs can be defeated before contact is made by thrusting the staff into the opponent's solar plexus to wind him, then smashing the staff across the side of his face to knock him to the ground.

A more advanced technique involves jabbing an opponent with the staff in the throat just as he is about to attack, then flipping the side of the staff into his face. The staff is then used to deliver a blow against the side of his knees. This causes him to buckle, which exposes the back of his neck, which allows the *coup de grace* to be delivered. All these movements should be completed in just over a second, but they require many hours of practice to perfect.

The *Bo*

Those special forces which include karate in their training programmes also often incorporate training in the use of the *bo*. The *bo* is a piece of hard wood approximately 2m (6ft) in length. Originally used as a walking stick and for prodding goats or cattle in the Far East, in the hands of a martial arts expert it is a formidable weapon.

The most common method of holding the *bo* is in the right or left hand with the staff going down the side of the leg. The hand is placed around the *bo* with the palm facing away from the body. The fingers themselves should be wrapped around the *bo*, with the forefinger extended and pointing downwards. The other arm is then brought across the chest and the hand clenches the staff with the palm facing away from the body. From this position the weapon can be used for attack or defence.

The great advantage with the *bo* is that its length means that most enemy attacks can be defeated before they come near the body. When an opponent swings a punch, for example, the end of the *bo* can be smashed into the attacker's ribs to knock him to the ground, where he can be finished off.

Punches can also be defeated by thrusting the end of the *bo* into the attacker's abdomen and then smashing it into the side of his face. This effectively disables the attacker.

Kicks can similarly be defeated by swinging the *bo* downwards across the foot as it kicks and then flipping the end of it into an attacker's groin. As he doubles over, the end of the *bo* is thrust into his throat and he is finished off with a quick smash to the neck and shoulders.

The *Yawara*

The *yawara*, too, is an extremely simple weapon, but in the right hands is lethal. It consists of a piece of hard wood 150-200mm (6-8in) long with blunt ends. It is normally used in conjunction with kicks and punches against the eyes, ears, groin and other vital areas. The *yawara* can be used to attack pressure points and nerves, and is so used by police officers in the Far East for the control of prisoners.

The correct grip for the *yawara* consists of holding the stick in the middle of the palm of the hand so that the end of the stick is approximately at the end of the forefinger. The last three fingers of the hand are then wrapped around the stick and the thumb pressed against its side. The forefinger is extended down to the end of the *yawara* for concealment and control.

Another grip consists of holding the *yawara* tightly with the fingers and then holding the thumb over one end for control, with around 50mm (2in) extending out the other side of the palm. Alternatively, the

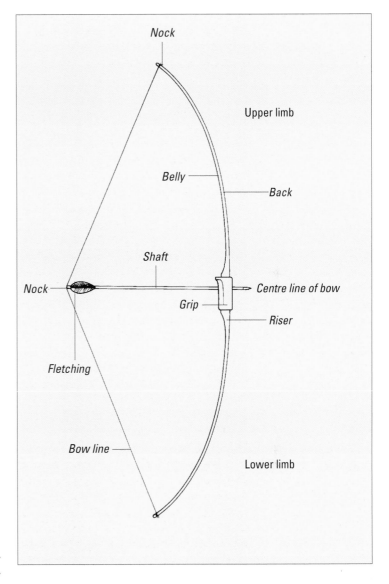

entire hand can be wrapped around the stick, leaving half of it pointing upwards. This is a particularly good hold for strikes against the throat and ears.

The *yawara* can be used with devastating effect in the attack. The eyes, bridge of the nose, ears and point below the ear at the top of the jaw can all be attacked. The size of the weapon bears no resemblance to its power. For example, even the largest attacker can be defeated by using several easy moves. In the first instance, pressing the point of the

Above: The constituent parts of a home-made bow. If a handle is fashioned, at least three-quarters of it should be below the weapon's centre line.

Above: A home-made 9mm submachine gun made from local materials. This example was seized from Loyalist terrorists by police in Northern Ireland.

yawara into the area above the collarbone will cause excruciating pain. Similarly, a large attacker can be pinioned against a wall with the *yawara* parallel to the ground by applying pressure against the top of the lips just under the nose. Simple but effective. The *yawara* can be used to break a grip on the wrist by simply smashing the end of it onto the back of the attacker's hand. This will result in several broken bones and an instant release of the grip!

Bows

Used by hunters and soldiers throughout history, the bow is a lethal and highly accurate weapon and one of the finest improvised weapons the elite forces soldier can create. In addition, it is also a relatively simple weapon to construct.

The first step is to pick the right wood. Hard, well seasoned, springy woods are the best, whereas soft woods such as fir, pine, larch and spruce should be avoided. The best woods are yew, elm, oak, rowan, birch, juniper and ironwood. Of these, yew is definitely the best. Yew should be handled with care, though, as the leaves, berry arils and sap contain taxine, a deadly nerve poison (Celtic warriors in ancient times used to dip their arrows in yew sap). Ideally the wood should be taken from a slim sapling growing in dense woodland. This is because trees growing close together have to 'shoot for the sun', and therefore grow slim and straight,

with just a few branches low on the trunk. The wood itself, once cut, needs to be worked on with a machete or heavy duty survival knife.

What length should the bow be? There are several factors that need to be taken into account. First, the longer the bow is the better it will resist a given pull. Second, if a fully made bow is shortened it will shoot further for the same draw, but will be harder to pull and is more likely to break. Normally, a bow drawing between 600 and 900mm (23 and 35in) should be sufficient. The bow should not bend in the middle – the central 300mm (12in) should be rigid. This implies that the bow should be at least 2m (6ft) long. It then needs to be seasoned.

The stave should be trimmed to the approximate size, leaving around 7mm (.25in) surplus in both thickness and breadth. In hot climates the wood can be left to dry naturally, but in cold climates it has to be dried over a fire. It can then be shaped by steaming over boiling water. Gentle pressure can be applied to mould the wood without creating any stresses.

The next step is to make the string. English bowmen in the Middle Ages used the stalks of the common stinging nettle. This takes a long time to master, so the special forces soldier has to improvise. Silk is ideal for a bow string because it stretches very little, though this material might be in short supply on the battlefield. Alternatively, nylon parachute cord can also be used. It stretches a little, but this can be taken up when bracing the bow.

Bracing, or putting the string on the bow, is extremely important. The hands should be placed thumbs-up on the back of the bow. The string should touch the thumb when correctly braced.

Like the bow, arrows can be made from locally available materials. The best woods are birch, ash, alder, willow, bamboo, oak, beech, elder and some reeds. The simplest, quickest and most versatile wood is bamboo. The arrow should be as straight as possible, as bends and kinks cause inaccuracy and wind resistance. Steam, or bending it over a warm stone, can be used to straighten it. Some woods can be straightened cold, by bending and holding them for a minute at the very least.

Flights can be fashioned from pieces of plastic or feathers (those of geese or large gliding birds are best). They are attached to the arrow by slitting the cane with two cuts. The first goes right the way through the arrow and the second is cut at 90 degrees to the first, going only halfway. The flights are inserted and secured at the end of the arrow with string or twine.

Shooting the Bow

A strong upper body is necessary for archery. The arm, which holds the bow in the centre, is held straight out in front of the body. The bow should be drawn back by the mid and forefinger, with the arrow notched in the string and resting between the two draw fingers. The two fingers should gently brush the side of the face as the shooter lines up his target. When shooting at a target it is important not to watch the end of the arrow. The eyes should be focused on the target all the time. When ready to shoot, the string is simply gently released.

The garrotte, a weapon usually associated with the execution of prisoners in some countries, is also used by special forces soldiers. It consists of about 1m (3ft) length of

wire firmly fastened to wooden handles at each end. The US Special Forces rules and regulations about close-quarter weapons has the following to say about the garrotte: 'If you are strong enough, you can use your arm power alone [to choke a sentry], otherwise loop the sentry's neck, turn back-to-back, and lever him off the ground by leaning forwards – until he stops moving. Warning: the tendency is to hurry, which can be a fatal error. Be certain the loop is around the neck, not his chin, and that he has stopped moving, not just stopped fighting for a minute.'

Russia's Spetsnaz soldiers are also trained in the use of the garrotte, only instead of a length of wire they use what is called a 'choking rope', which is simply a length of paracord. The length of rope between the hands is 300-500mm (12-20in). The method for neutralising the enemy sentry is the same as that described for the US Special Forces above.

Other Improvised Weapons

Almost anything can be use as a weapon if the user is confident enough and has the will to carry out an attack. For example, a sock one-third full of sand and tied at the end can be used to stun an enemy. Called a blackjack, this weapon can be used to hit an opponent hard behind the ear.

KGB personnel are taught to use whatever is to hand. An ordinary chair, for example, will be sufficient: 'After hitting him in the face with the chair, you can kick him in the shin, knee or crotch.'

The teeth are also excellent weapons for close-quarter combat. When grappling with an enemy they can be used to tear the nose, throat or ears.

Below: The garrotte, simple and deadly. Its use is taught to many elite soldiers around the world, including the US Green Berets and Russia's Spetsnaz.

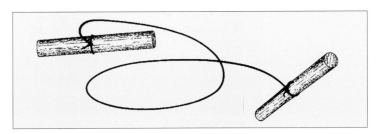

CHAPTER 5

THROWING & TENSION WEAPONS

Despite Hollywood folklore, the main weapon of a special forces soldier is not a composite bow. The reality is that elite troops rarely make use of tension weapons, save for survival purposes, and although some hostage-rescue units have crossbows, these are more for show than use.

There are very few occasions when elite troops use throwing or tension weapons. The reasons are obvious: their range is limited compared to firearms, as is their accuracy. In addition, carrying arrows and the like is yet another burden for elite troops, who, often on foot, are invariably already overloaded with kit. That said, there are two occasions when special forces soldiers might use these types of weapons (see Chapter 4). First, when they have to improvise them during a survival scenario. Second, some hostage-rescue units train in the use of modern composite bows and crossbows to assist them on operations.

All elite troops are taught to use the knife to varying degrees (see Chapter 3), though this usually entails using it to stab and slash. Throwing a knife is a different matter, and requires many hours of training. Russia's Spetsnaz soldiers are among the finest in the world when it comes to throwing knives, but can be considered very rare among the special forces brotherhood. Their basic training includes

Left: A US soldier in Vietnam aims a flaming arrow at a suspected enemy location. Usually flamethrowers were used to burn out the enemy.

knife throwing: the minimum standard demanded of recruits when throwing a knife from six paces is three hits on target. Five hits is considered excellent. But why train soldiers to throw knives? The Spetsnaz training manual is quite specific on this matter: 'Soldiers can use, for the most part, basic cold weapons for throwing at a target: knives, bayonets, axes and some pointed or edged items and pieces of equipment. The penetrating (killing) force of a knife thrown is almost doubled. Experiments have shown that a stab down into a board goes in about sixteen to seventeen millimetres, and a knife penetrates to about twenty-seven to twenty-eight millimetres.'

The first thing recruits are shown is how to hold a knife for throwing. Eastern elite forces use the following method: the knife is held so that it is balanced on the forefinger of whatever hand it is being thrown from. This is the point at which the knife can be controlled most easily (a good knife should be balanced properly). The knife is then thrown in an overhand motion.

Russian and Western elite troops use a slightly different method when throwing a knife; the weapon is gripped for throwing by holding its handle or blade. It is thrown from behind the head, like a grenade. When throwing the knife the feet, back, shoulders and arm all come into play in sequence. The throwing hand undertakes the decisive movement, with the opposite foot forward.

Below: A typical military fighting knife. Knives are rarely used for throwing by elite soldiers, Spetsnaz troops being the exception.

The most powerful throw is one from behind the head. The throw's distance depends on how high the grip is on the blade (the sharp edge is always away from the body).

If an opponent is closing, the knife is thrown with a grip closer to the tip of the blade. The greater the distance, the grip has to be placed farther up the blade. Typically, five to six paces is regarded as ideal for ensuring a hit. An opponent should be hit before he has a chance to duck, which is achieveable at six paces. Any farther and the enemy has more time to avoid the strike.

Knife Blades

The blade itself should be thrown in a sweeping movement from behind the head, with the free hand held out forward. The knife should be released at eye level, and the crucial part is guiding the weapon at the decisive moment when it leaves the hand. The thrower has to extend himself into the throw. As the Spetsnaz manual states; 'This fundamental part of the technique has to be developed through repeated practice with and without a weapon at the beginning of throwing training.'

One unusual weapon believed to be unique to Spetsnaz is the 'firing knife'. This is a hand-held device, which looks rather like a heavy knife and can be used as such. But if the blade is pointed at a target, and a catch released, a powerful spring fires the blade at the target. It is supposedly effective up to about 5m (16ft) distant. The usefulness of such a weapon must be limited, but it could be handy for silent killing, especially for a swimmer or frogman just leaving the water, where a firearm would be of no use.

Though spears in a military context are improvised weapons, they are included here because they are throwing weapons. They are used by special forces soldiers almost entirely for survival purposes, but are nevertheless lethal weapons, which can be used against opponents if need be.

The easiest spear that can be made is the so-called 'self spear'. This is simply a straight

piece of hard, natured wood with a sharpened point. The hardening of the point can be improved over a fire and by fashioning it into a leaf-shaped blade. In a survival situation, where the soldier is hunting game to eat, the spear's cutting edge should be wide enough to cause maximum bleeding but not so wide that it prevents the spear penetrating the vital organs. The same is true when attacking human beings. The point is therefore definitely the most important part of the spear.

Throwing spears are obviously used at a distance. They therefore need to be light so that they can fly fast. In addition, the point needs to be of such a design that it will penetrate with the force of the throw (to aid retention in the target, throwing spear points are often barbed).

Throwing Spears

Throwing a spear is not like throwing a javelin. There is no 'run up' to the target or 'pulling back' before the throw. The spear should be launched immediately at the target. The throwing arm is slowly drawn back like a coiled spring, being careful not to draw it back beyond the shoulder. If it is pulled back beyond the shoulder the thrower's body will have to be turned. It is far better to use the resistance of the shoulder as a buffer, from which all the throwing force is generated. When it is time for the throw, the spear is cast like a dart in one explosive moment. The movement should be followed through with the arm.

Whether used against animals or humans, it is often advantageous to make the spear fly faster. An ancient method of making throwing spears fly faster is to use a spear thrower, called a *woomera* by the Australian Aborigines. This is basically an extension of the arm, and thus gives greater leverage. It consists of a length of wood 450-1000mm (18-39in) long with a notch at one end, into which fits the end of the throwing spear. It is operated with a flicking wrist action, and the spear is projected at great speed. The throw-

er follows through with his throwing arm to aid accuracy.

These two weapons are lightweight, easy to use and deadly. In the popular imagination (fuelled mostly by the Rambo series of films) they are used by all elite soldiers to kill the enemy. Nothing could be further from the truth. Nevertheless, crossbows in particular are used by some elite units, so they and compound bows will be discussed briefly.

Compound bows usually consist of a belly made of aluminium and limbs constructed from fibre glass. At the end of each limb is a pulley wheel, attached to which are three strings, which run to the other pulley wheel. One of the strings is the draw cord, while the other two assist in the draw and producing the force of the arrow's propulsion. Drawing the string back is easy because of the pulley effect of the two assisting strings. When the string is released, the pulley strings also increase the propulsive force, thus increasing the speed of the arrow. Compound bows are relatively easy to master; because of the pulleys they do not tire the user as much as traditional bows, such as a longbow.

The arrows fired by compound bows are not made of wood. They are constructed either from lightweight metal such as tin or a similar alloy, or composite materials such as carbon fibre. This makes them extremely light and fast when loosed from a bow.

Above: One reason why elite troops hardly ever throw knives is that they are in effect throwing a valuable weapon away, notwithstanding that it may find its target.

However, there are several problems with these types of arrows. First, the carbon models are very delicate. They can be deflected by branches, even leaves, and if they glance hard targets they can shatter or bend. Second, and more important, there can be problems with light arrows from powerful bows when striking the target. In the United States, for example, compound bows are often used for hunting game as their range and lethality make them ideal for shooting animals. However, some hunters have reported that arrows fired from compound bows with large draw weights have occasionally gone straight through animals such as bears and deer, with the target hardly noticing! For an elite soldier in a one-on-one situation this would be potentially fatal. A third problem with compound bows is the noise they make. The loud 'thwack' they make when shooting negates their use as a silenced weapon, and identifies the general location of the firer to the enemy.

Modern crossbows suffer from similar problems: they are noisy, can be heavy and their arrows can be deflected and shatter before they reach the target. That said, a number of special forces units include crossbows in their armouries for unspecified 'special jobs'. Belgium's *Escardron Special D'Intervention* (Special Intervention Squadron) is one of the world's top hostage-rescue units. Among the weapons it uses is a lightweight crossbow fitted with a telescopic sight. But what is this weapon actually used for?

A hint as to the uses for crossbows by modern elite forces is provided by Portugal's *Grupo De Operacoes Especias* (GOE), the Portuguese national police counter-terrorist and hostage-rescue unit. The members of the unit are trained in the use of the crossbow; during simulated aircraft assaults GOE operatives have been observed firing crossbows at dummies representing terrorists holding hostages on the tarmac. However, it is difficult to envisage these weapons being used during actual assaults, especially when it takes several seconds to load another bolt after the first has been fired.

Other Weapons

Many objects that have blades or points can be used as throwing weapons. However, they require hours of practice to perfect technique before they can be used with any confidence of striking the target. Axes, for example, have been used throughout history as throwing weapons. When thrown at a target the axe itself should make one full turn before striking. Targets farther away will require at least two full turns of the axe, though this demands many hours of practice to perfect.

Right: A French Foreign Legionnaire practising shooting a modern crossbow during jungle training in Brazil. Such weapons have limited military uses, having short range and being bulky.

DEADLY FIREPOWER

CHAPTER 6

GRENADES & FLAME-THROWERS

Grenades and grenade launchers are an essential part of the special forces arsenal, being used for a number of tasks, such as demolitions, killing enemy personnel and as signalling aids. Even flamethrowers are used by some units to flush enemy troops out of fortified positions.

L ike conventional soldiers, all special forces troops receive instruction in the use of hand grenades. This chapter will discuss the types of grenade used by special forces troops, how they are used and the grenades used for hostage-rescue operations. It will also look at flamethrowers.

There are dozens of different grenade models in service throughout the world, but all work according to the same principles and contain the same constituent elements. A modern hand grenade consists of three main parts: a pyrotechnic fuse and detonator, usually set in train by the action of a spring-loaded striker on a percussion cap; and a high-explosive filling encased within a fragmentation body of wire or steel. In general they weigh between 140 and 150g (4.9 and 17.5oz), which means they can be thrown up to a range of about 30m (100ft).

The fuse sets fire to a train of powder that burns at a controlled rate (this stops the grenade exploding until several seconds after it is thrown). Some fuses burn into an igniting cap, which sets off the

Left: A French Foreign Legionnaire flamethrower in action during a training exercise, an image which gives an idea of the power of this weapon.

fillers (igniting fuses), while others burn into a blasting or detonating cap (detonating fuses). There are other fuses which do not splutter or smoke while the delay fuse is burning – these are known as silent fuses.

A grenade's filling is usually an explosive such as TNT, although special chemical compounds are used for white phosphorus, smoke or tear gas. Grenade bodies are shaped according to their type. The body of a fragmentation grenade, for example, is usually shaped like a lemon, whereas 'chemical' grenades usually have cylindrical bodies.

US and British Throwing Styles

Elite units such as the US Navy's SEALs are instructed to use a grenade thus: the soldier needs to hold the grenade so that the fingers of the throwing hand pass around the body of the grenade and the palm is over the safety lever. The safety pin is removed before the grenade is thrown. When the grenade leaves the hand, the safety lever is thrown clear of the grenade by the action of the striking spring, forcing the striker through its arc. The striker continues through its arc until it strikes the primer, igniting it. Then the primer ignites the powder train, which burns for a pre-determined time before reaching the detonator, which ignites the filler.

Right: The standard-issue British Army L2 fragmentation grenade, which is used by the SAS and SBS. It has a 4.3-second delay.

Special forces troops have different ways of throwing grenades. American units such as the Rangers, Green Berets and SEALs are taught to throw a grenade like a baseball, 'using the throwing motion that is most natural to the individual'. US instructors recommend giving the grenade a spinning motion in flight by allowing the grenade to roll off the fingertips with a snapping motion of the wrist. This reportedly improves both accuracy and distance.

British units such as the SAS, SBS, Royal Marines and Paras are taught to swing their throwing arms upwards and to release the grenade when the arm reaches its highest point (like bowling a cricket ball).

Kneeling and Lying Positions

Both the above throwing styles are from a standing position, but in combat the target may be in urban areas, jungle or similar terrain, where the user may only have a fleeting view of the enemy. It is therefore important to be able to throw a grenade from a variety of positions. Kneeling behind a low wall, for example, it is still perfectly feasible to throw a grenade, though it is not possible to get as much distance as from the standing position. The user should kneel on the knee nearest the target and extend the other leg slightly to the rear. The grenade is held at chest height, the pin removed, then the grenade thrown with a natural motion, at the same time pushing off with the rear foot to give added power to the throw. As the distance at which casualties can be caused can be as much as 190m (620ft) from the point of burst on hard ground, it is important for the thrower to lie behind cover when the grenade is thrown.

From the crouch position, normally for use in built-up areas, woods or jungle, a grenade can be thrown short distances under low-hanging trees or into enemy pillboxes. The grenade is thrown with an underhand motion, being allowed to roll off the fingertips. Then the thrower lies down for cover.

From the prone position itself it is difficult to throw a grenade. However, it may be necessary when pinned down by enemy fire. The thrower lies on his back with his body perpendicular to the thrower-target line and the throwing arm away from the target. The grenade is held chest high and the pin removed with a twisting-pulling motion. The right leg is cocked with the foot braced against the ground and the throwing arm is brought back. If possible, grasp a solid object with the left hand to improve accuracy and distance. When throwing the grenade, push with the rear foot and roll onto the stomach and duck the head.

Types of Grenade

All elite units use a wide variety of grenade types, both for use against the enemy and for identification and screening purposes. Fragmentation grenades (as mentioned above, these are usually lemon-shaped). The British L2 and American M26 are examples of this type. On detonation their bodies break up and metal fragments are thrown out at high velocity in all directions. The design of the grenades ensures that the fragments are of equal size and are large enough to cause casualties within a radius of 30m (100ft).

Incendiary grenades usually consist of a body of smooth metal with no vents, a ther-

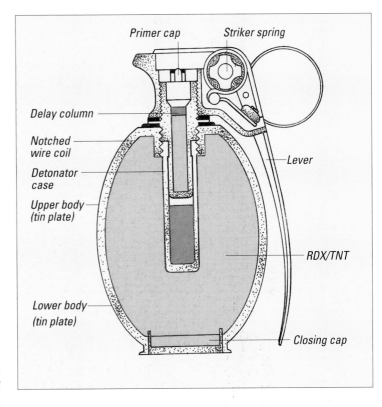

mite filler and an igniting-type fuse. When the filler is ignited, it burns with a white-hot flame that increases to a temperature of 2388 degrees C for 30-35 seconds. These types of

Above: The components of the L2 anti-personnel grenade.

Left: US Marines in Vietnam, February 1969. Note the baseball-type throwing style being used to launch the grenade.

grenade tend to be placed rather than thrown, and because of the great heat they generate are ideal for destroying enemy ordnance and machinery. During a raid, for example, they could be attached to stationary aircraft with devastating effect.

White phosphorus grenades have cylindrical bodies similar in size to burning-type grenades. However, the body is made of a heavier sheet metal than other smoke-type grenades. The filler is white phosphorus, and the fuse has a delay of four to five seconds. When the filler comes into contact with air, it burns with a dense white irritant smoke, which blinds the enemy. When it comes into contact with skin white phosphorus also causes severe burns. Upon detonation the filler is spread over an area of around 14m (45ft). Smoke grenades, the last category, can produce smoke of various colours, and are used for signalling and screening purposes.

Grenades have many uses, but they must be employed correctly to achieve the maximum effect. In house-to-house fighting, for example, it is tactically sound to clear houses by first lobbing in one or two grenades before a section or squad storms the building. As soon as the grenades have detonated the men storm into the room and spray it with fire. A similar tactic is used by hostage-rescue units when equipped with stun grenades (see below). One important point stressed to elite soldiers is the need to 'post' grenades when engaged in close-quarter fighting, as opposed to throwing them. Infantrymen in training are taught that their rifle is their best friend, but, when clearing a house, the grenade replaces the rifle in the favouritism stakes. Its explosive strength is increased by the small enclosed spaces, and it provides a quicker source of firepower in a situation where speed is survival.

When clearing rooms elite troops are taught not to use the door handle, as it could be booby-trapped, and its moving warns any enemy within that someone is about to enter. Instead, they are instructed to use a burst of automatic fire to shoot off the lock, then to kick the door open. The first thing into the room is the grenade, but the user has pulled its pin and waited for a couple of seconds, known as letting it 'cook off', before he throws it in. This stops any enemy troops in the room picking it up or catching it and throwing it back. Users also have to be aware of very thin plaster walls – grenade fragments can go straight through them and into friendly troops.

Right: An American inshore patrol craft during the Vietnam War. The soldier bottom right is holding an M79 grenade launcher.

Grenade users must also be wary of using them in wooded terrain. For example, if thrown there is a real danger of them bouncing back off trees. The have to be placed accurately, and if the enemy is well dug-in, then grenades are always more of a danger to the user.

Grenade Mix

On actual operations all elite troops will carry a variety of grenade types. The experiences of the US Green Berets, SEALs and Rangers in Vietnam led to a number of rules regarding the use of grenades by special forces. First, there was the grenade mix. Each member of a patrol sent into enemy territory carried fragmentation, CS and white phosphorus grenades. It was discovered that fragmentation grenades are best for inflicting casualties, whereas the CS models are ideal for stopping or slowing down pursuing enemy units (CS gas also stops dogs from following a trail in wet weather as the CS powder dissipates due to the moisture in the air). White phosphorus grenades have a great psychological effect on the enemy, whereas incendiary grenades are used almost solely for the destruction of equipment.

Smoke grenades are mostly carried in the backpack or bergen because they are not for fighting but for identification or masking purposes. It was soon discovered that grenades carried on webbing attracted enemy fire (one successful shot to a single grenade could wipe out the whole section), therefore they are always attached to the lower part of the webbing or harness.

A team escaping from the enemy can also use its grenades. For example, CS grenades thrown out to the flanks and rear will slow any pursuers. Similarly, CS grenades can be used at night when the enemy is near: they do not give the team's position away and they will confuse the enemy. Once the gas starts to envelop the enemy he will often panic, especially if he has no gas mask. If the hostile troops have gas masks they will put them on, but this means they will not be able

Left: The combination which solved the problem of the M79 being a dedicated weapon: the M203 grenade launcher, seen here attached to an M16 assault rifle.

to see so clearly. All this activity helps the friendly team to escape.

Grenade Launchers

Since the 1960s grenade launchers have become an important part of the weapons make-up of special forces teams. At a stroke they allow individual members of a patrol to propel a projectile up to a range of around 300m (970ft). In addition, and perhaps more importantly, they allow teams to lay down a large amount of firepower at short notice – invaluable if ambushed. They can be used against bunkers and other strongpoints, they can be fired through windows and doors, and they can be attached to assault rifles, making them significant force multipliers.

There are two major drawbacks to grenade launchers, though. First, the grenade travels in a straight line, which means it cannot be 'dropped' behind cover, unlike a grenade thrown by hand. Second, projectiles launched by grenade launchers tend to be two-thirds fuse and only one-third explosive. Nevertheless, grenade launchers are here to stay as far as elite teams are concerned, and

Above: The Russian 30mm AGS-17 grenade launcher, which was used by Spetsnaz troops during the war in Afghanistan.

the first enter service was the US Army's M79 model.

The M79, nicknamed 'bloop gun', was designed as a close-support weapon for infantry, effectively plugging the gap between the hand grenade and the mortar. It was a single-shot, shoulder-fired weapon which broke open to allow the 40mm grenade 'cartridge' to be loaded into the breech. In flight the grenade was stabilised by means of fins and the spinning caused by the rifling in the barrel. The grenade travelled at a speed of 75mps (244fps). As it spun, weights in the fuse mechanism armed the grenade after it had flown 30m (100ft), after which it would detonate on impact. This meant that the grenade could not be accidentally set off and kept the firer beyond its fragmentation radius.

For close-range work the US Army developed two shells, one containing buckshot and the other dart-like flechettes. The M79 could also fire CS grenades, smoke grenades and airburst projectiles. After its use in countless encounters by Green Berets, SEALs and Rangers, the British SAS also took to the M79 and used it during its campaign in Oman in the 1970s.

The one problem with the M79 was that it was a dedicated weapon, i.e. its user usually carried only a handgun in addition to the launcher. He was therefore almost defenceless until he loaded another grenade into the breech. This problem led to the development of the M203 grenade launcher, which satisfied the requirement for a grenade launcher/rifle package.

The M203 launcher is a single-shot, sliding barrel, breech-loaded, shoulder-fired weapon designed for attachment to the M16 series of assault rifles. It consists of a receiver constructed of high-strength aluminium alloy, a barrel made from the same material, and a handguard. It is normally clipped underneath the barrel of the M16. The M203 is loaded by sliding its barrel forward in the receiver and inserting a grenade manually. The barrel then slides back to lock in the closed position, ready to fire. After firing, a forward movement of the barrel ejects the spent cartridge. The maximum range is around 400m (1300ft), against area targets 350m (1140ft), and against point targets 150m (490ft). The M203 can fire a variety of grenades, including high explosive and buckshot. This means that special forces troops can take on light armour, enemy personnel and lay down smoke rounds as well. The M203 is used by special forces units which receive American equipment, most notably the British SAS, Israeli units, South Korea, Indonesia, Thailand and Turkey.

The special forces of Russia have a similar weapon in the 40mm GP-25 rifle-mounted grenade launcher, which entered Russian service in 1984 in Afghanistan. It can be mounted under the handguard of virtually any AKM or AK-74 series assault rifle. The GP-25 fires two types of grenade: the VOG-25 and VOG-25P. Both are steel fragmentation grenades, but the VOG-25 has a nose-impact fuse capable of operating in snow or soft ground. The VOG-25P is a 'bouncing' fragmentation grenade which strikes the ground before being thrown upwards to a height of 1.5m (5ft), where it detonates to spread anti-personnel fragments over a lethal radius of at least 6m (20ft).

Grenade Launchers in Action

How do elite teams use grenade launchers? In general they are favoured as a powerful anti-ambush weapon, which was the main role of the American M79 (see above). Grenade launchers are designed for ease of use. The cartridges themselves, for example, are designed so that the grenade launchers are controllable and consistent at all times. In the American 40mm projectile this is called the High-Low Pressure System, whereby the propellant charge is confined inside a small chamber in the base of the cartridge case. This chamber has carefully calculated holes; when the cap is fired the charge explodes inside the chamber and creates very high pressures. Normally these pressures would blow the grenade out of the weapon at great speed and place great stress on the weapon breech. However, the high-pressure gas is confined to the special chamber in the cartridge case; via the holes it 'bleeds' into the empty space of the rest of the case. Here it expands and drops in pressure so that the grenade leaves the barrel at

a reduced velocity. This being the case, the stress on the weapon is not excessive and so the barrel can be thin and lightweight.

Special forces troops have always favoured weapons that are lightweight, hence the popularity of the M203. However, on occasion they have to call upon heavier firepower. With regard to grenades this has meant the adoption of automatic grenade launchers. These are in effect 'machine guns' firing 40mm grenades up to long ranges. Produced in the USA, Singapore, Spain, Germany, China and Russia, they have awesome firepower. For defence of a static base they are ideal: for destroying enemy bunkers they are also useful. During the 1991 Gulf War, British SAS teams with Land Rover vehicles had American Mark 19 grenade launchers mounted on their vehicles. This air-cooled, blowback-type weapon can fire high-explosive anti-armour and anti-personnel grenades to a range of 1600m (5200ft). Fed from a 32- or 50-round ammunition container, it has a rate of fire of 325-374 rounds per minute and weighs 34kg (75lb).

The AGS-17

In Afghanistan Spetsnaz teams often had difficulty in dislodging *Mujahedeen* units from mountain bunkers. The solution to their problem was the 30mm AGS-17 automatic grenade launcher. It fires fragmentation grenades which spread fragments over a lethal radius of 7m (23ft) out to 1700m (5500ft) at a rate of 65 rounds per minute. Developed by the Russians in the late 1960s and early 1970s, it did not gain fame until its use during the war in Afghanistan. Issued to infantry companies, including Spetsnaz teams, at a rate of two per company, they were ideal for laying down heavy fire to cover an advance (they were also mounted on vehicles and helicopters). When mounted on its tripod the AGS-17 weighs over 30kg (66lb), with a 300-round magazine weighing a further 14.5kg (32lb). While this is prohibitively heavy for foot patrols, Spetsnaz patrols air-landed on mountains by helicopter could easily establish grenade launcher bases to support their assault.

One kind of grenade that is used almost exclusively by elite units throughout the world is the non-lethal stun grenade. Designed for use in hostage-rescue operations, it was developed by the British SAS in the 1970s. Each team member will be equipped with a number of grenades to facilitate clearance of areas which may contain terrorists. During an assault to clear a building, for example, it is customary for the hostage-rescue team to divide into two-man elements, each pair having been previously given specific areas to clear. The drill for clearing a room is simple: kick in the door or blow off the hinges with shotgun rounds, throw in a stun grenade, wait for it to detonate and then rush in and neutralise any terrorists with small-arms fire. Crucial to the success of the drill is the stun grenade. It is essentially a diversionary device which produces a blinding flash and loud bang, hence its nickname 'flash bang'. It literally stuns an opponent into inaction for a second or two, thus allowing hostage-rescue troops a couple

of seconds in order to close and kill all the terrorists in the immediate area.

There are several types of grenade on the market, including a German model, which is a flare and sound grenade, which produces a bright white flash that lasts for 15 seconds. Another one is a multi-report model, which issues eight loud bangs in quick succession. How loud is loud? Leroy Thompson, an ex-Green Beret, attests to the power of stun grenades while taking part in a simulated hostage-rescue mission: 'I have been inside a room acting as a "hostage" during an exercise in which stun grenades exploded less than five feet from me and though the 2,000,000 plus candle power and 200 plus decibels certainly did disorient me – even though I knew they were coming.'

Flamethrowers have traditionally been used by conventional infantry and armoured units, and are seldom employed by special forces troops. For one thing, the weight of a flamethrowing device often precludes its inclusion in the kit of a special forces team, especially if it is travelling on foot. That said, there are two formations which do make use

Right: Spetsnaz troops make use of the LPO-50 flamethrower shown here. It has a range of 70m (230ft).

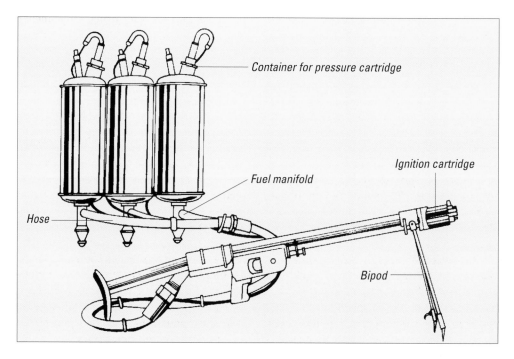

Container for pressure cartridge

Ignition cartridge

Fuel manifold

Hose

Bipod

of flamethrowers in their operations. They are the US Marines and Russia's Spetsnaz.

A traditional type of flamethrower used by Spetsnaz troops is the LPO-50 model. This consists of three tanks, a hose and a gun to project the flame. Wires from the three chambers are combined in a harness, which is fastened to the hose and attached to the gun. Each of the tanks is fitted with a one-way valve, which prevents fuel flowing from one tank to another. There are three slow-burning pyrotechnic cartridges below the muzzle of the gun, and it is these which provide the ignition of the fuel.

The LPO-50 Flamethrower

When the trigger is pressed, energy is supplied by a power pack of four 1.5 volt cells to one of the ignition cartridges and simultaneously to one of the tank pressurising cartridges. Pressure from the latter drives fuel from the tank through its non-return valve into the manifold, then through the hose to the gun, where it is ignited by the pyrotechnic charge. Each tank's capacity is 3.3 litres (0.7gal), allowing a flame burst of two to three seconds. Depending on the type of fuel used (thickened or unthickened), the LPO-50 has a range of up to 70m (230ft). A disadvantage with the system, though, is that it weighs 23kg (51lb) loaded.

A much more advanced Russian flamethrowing system, and one currently in Spetsnaz use, is the RPO-A Schmel Rocket Infantry flamethrower. Actually it is not a flamethrower but a rocket-propelled incendiary/blast projectile launcher. It uses advanced fuel-air explosive techniques, which, on detonation, create deflagration as the warhead cloud bursts. This produces a blast effect in addition to the high temperatures generated.

The latest version of the RPO-A combines the fuel-air warhead with a small hollow charge, which can penetrate light armour or buildings to allow the main warhead to detonate inside the target, thereby increasing the weapon's destructive effects. Against strong-

Left: An LPO-50 flamethrower in action. Used by the Russians in Afghanistan, it was very effective against enemy cave strongholds.

points it is an excellent weapon; Spetsnaz units found it ideal for flushing out *Mujahedeen* from their cave strongholds (or rather incinerating them inside the caverns).

The RPO-A is a single-tube launcher usually carried in pairs to facilitate their use as a backpack. For use the two tubes are separated and a sight flipped up on the tube to be fired. Firing is from the shoulder, with a folding pistol grip, trigger assembly and forward grip under the muzzle. After firing, the launcher tube is discarded. The 93mm (3.6in) projectile warhead consists of 2.1kg (4.6lb) of 'thermobaric' flammable mixture, 2.1kg (4.6lb) of incendiary substance and 2.3kg (5lb) of an incendiary-smoke mixture.

Maximum range is around 1000m (3250ft), though the sights are only calibrated to 600m (1960ft). When detonated inside a structure the RPO-A's lethal and destructive effects will cover an area of 80 square metres (860 square feet), while in the open the lethal area will cover an area of 150 square metres (540 square feet).

In the West, the US Marines use the 66mm M202A2 multi-shot portable flame weapon. It consists of a shoulder-fired, four-tube rocket launcher and a pre-loaded four-round incendiary rocket clip which slides into the launcher tubes. The weapon can be fired standing, sitting or kneeling.

CHAPTER 7

SNIPING

For the elite sniper, taking the shot is only one part of the mission. He has to have expert camouflage, concealment and movement skills to get into a position from where he can fire. He also needs to know what to fire at and the effects the wind and range will have on his shot.

This chapter will examine two aspects of special forces sniping: marksmanship in the field and hostage-rescue sniping, the latter an area that is becoming increasingly important to elite units. In the field it is the sniper's task to kill an opponent with a single shot while remaining unseen. But before he pulls the trigger, a sniper must be able to move into the best position in order to take the shot. This means he must be a master of the art of camouflage and concealment. Camouflage involves blending in with the local environment, which usually entails covering the face and hands in camouflage cream, attaching natural foliage to the uniform and wrapping the rifle in hessian or similar material (some rifles, such as the US Marines Corps' M40, are made with a variety of camouflaged stocks). There are other preparations that a sniper must undertake before his mission. His kit, for example, must not rattle or snag when he is moving. This involves taping loose items that are hanging or slack. In addition, all clothing must be soft and flexible – a starched uniform makes a noise – and baggy clothes can become snagged on undergrowth and branches, thus they have to be tied at the thigh and ankles. Once in the field the sniper has to obey certain rules to ensure the approach to a firing position is successful. All movement is made, where possible, in conditions that will obscure the sniper's presence, such as at night, or in fog, smoke or haze. The terrain itself is both the sniper's friend and foe. Though it provides cover, it can also present problems. Moving through tall grass in a straight line, for example, causes the foliage to wave

Left: A French Foreign Legion sniper team equipped with a Barrett M82A1 sniper rifle. This 0.5in-calibre gun has a range of 1500m (4900ft).

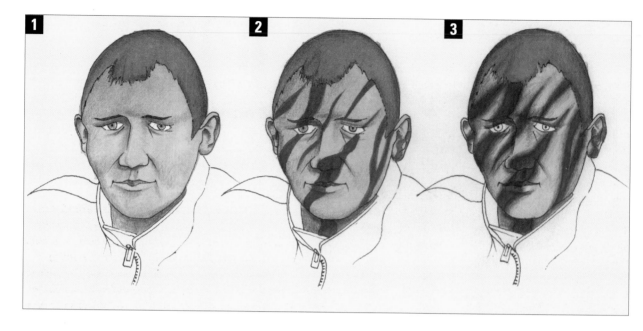

Above: Applying face camouflage. The sniper must first mix spit and camouflage cream into his hands and then rub the mixture over his face, neck and ears (1). He then uses more cream to break up the shape and outline of the face's features (2). Finally, earth and green colours are applied and rubbed over the face (3).

unnaturally. The sniper therefore has to change his direction frequently, and if possible move only when the wind is blowing the grass. Steep slopes and loose, stony areas are dangerous to cross because they may result in accidental movements or sounds that can betray a presence. Similarly, ridge lines and areas devoid of cover must be avoided at all times as they will reveal a sniper's silhouette to the enemy.

Elite snipers utilise a number of movement techniques to reach the firing position. The low crawl, for example, is used to move over ground with poor cover, where speed is not essential and when there is a high probability of being spotted by the enemy. The sniper lies flat and keeps his head down all the time, holding the rifle sling with one hand at the upper sling swivel, with the rifle body on top of the forearm and the butt dragging on the ground. The arms and right leg are pushed forward, and the body is moved forward by pulling with the arms and pushing with the right leg. The body is kept flat at all times.

The high crawl is used in situations where there is adequate cover and concealment, poor visibility and where more speed is

required. The trunk of the body is kept clear of the ground, with the weight on the forearms and the lower legs. The rifle is cradled on the top of the arms, with the muzzle off the ground. The sniper moves by alternately advancing left elbow and right knee. The actual movements are short, with the head kept low. When closer to the enemy, a sniper can use the silent walk.

Silent walking is undertaken with extreme care, being used mainly at night or in heavy cover. The sniper balances on one foot as he lifts the other high enough to clear brush or grass. The forward foot is then put down gently, feeling with the toe for a solid footing before putting the weight on it. The body's weight is then shifted forward onto the forward foot. Then the process is repeated with the other foot. At night the sniper will hold his rifle with one hand, using the other to feel for any obstacles.

When it comes to assuming a prone position from the silent walk, the sniper will crouch down slowly, hold his weapon under his arm and feel for an appropriate spot with his other hand. Having found a suitable position, the sniper will then rest his weight on his free hand and the opposite knee. The free leg is then extended to the rear, keeping it clear of the ground until the toe finds a clear spot. He then rolls into the prone position.

Stalking is the sniper's art of moving unseen into a firing position that will ensure a first-round kill when he fires, and then withdrawing undetected. The stalk requires much practice to perfect, plus the level of fieldcraft skills possessed by special forces soldiers. The first thing that a sniper will do is undertake a thorough reconnaissance of the area. If this is not possible then maps and aerial photographs will be studied intensely. The best area for a firing position is chosen, along with a line of advance. The selection of the route will depend on a number of factors. The US Marines' sniper manual lists the following points to be considered when choosing a route to the firing position: the availability of natural cover and any dead space; the position and frequency of any natural and artificial obstacles; likely points along the route from which observations can be made; the whereabouts of known or possible enemy locations; the general method of movement likely for each stage of the approach; and the route of the withdrawal, which should be different from that of the approach.

Once in position, the elite forces sniper will have to detect and then select his target accordingly. The enemy can help him detect a target, especially if his camouflage or movement discipline is poor. Though enemy observation posts and firing positions can be well-camouflaged, careful, detailed searching can reveal their whereabouts to the sniper. Similarly, any reflection off glasses, binoculars, metal, optical devices and pools of water, though lasting only a fraction of a

Below: British Royal Marine Commandos apply face camouflage before a stalking exercise. Camouflage skills are vital to the success of sniper missions in the field.

Above: A sniper in the field has to ensure his movements do not disturb foliage in a telltale manner, which will reveal his position to the enemy.

second, can betray the location of the enemy. Unusual colours that stand out against their backgrounds could be an enemy site, as could anything that looks out of place or unusual. In addition, if combat is taking place around them, snipers can use the so-called 'crack and thump' method to locate enemy positions.

When an enemy rifle is fired the first sound the sniper will hear will be the crack of the bullet flying at supersonic speed as it passes overhead (more than one crack may be heard if the bullet passes several objects). This is always followed by a lower sounding thump (the discharge of the rifle). At shorter ranges the two sounds will be close together, while at long ranges the sounds are farther apart. With training, a sniper can determine the distance. For example, a one-second lapse between crack and thump equates to a weapon around 630m (1800ft) away, where-as a half-second lapse equates to 315m

(900ft). Once the range has been determined, by watching in the direction of the sound the sniper may be able to identify the location of the enemy position.

In the event of detecting multiple enemy locations, the elite sniper has to weigh the consequences of shooting at a number of targets, which may reveal his position. But what to shoot at? All snipers have a list of key targets; these are officers, non-commissioned officers, scouts, crew-served weapons personnel, tank commanders, communications personnel and enemy snipers. When these targets present themselves the sniper will usually fire. However, he will be aware of range considerations. A shot is usually fired against a target located 550-900m (1800-3000ft) away. He will rarely fire at a target which is at a range of 270m (900ft) or below for risk of being spotted.

Taking the shot is at the end of a long process for both the sniper and his rifle. We have discussed the sniper's preparations above. But what about the rifle? The different types of sniper rifles currently available will be discussed below, but an essential part of any rifle are the sights through which the sniper takes his aim. These are usually matched to the rifle at the factory, with their serial number corresponding to the serial of the gun. Telescopic sights magnify the image. The Redfield telescopic sight, for example, used by the US Marines, can magnify the image by a minimum of three times and a maximum of nine, and is adjusted using a power selection ring. In general, lower power is required in poor light conditions, as it gives a wider field of view. The higher the power, on the other hand, the more pronounced the movement of the crosshairs, though the higher power does allow the sniper to see into dense foliage.

Every rifle, no matter how precisely engineered, fires slightly differently, and all need their sights zeroed to ensure that a round fired will go through the centre of the target. Bullets do not travel in straight lines on their journey from the muzzle to the target, but rather travel in a vertical arc called the trajectory. The farther a round has to go to hit a target, the higher the trajectory it must make. Thus sights have to be adjusted to take into account range. One way to zero a rifle is by boresighting. The rifle has its bolt removed and is placed on a bed of sandbags on the range. The sniper looks through the breech and down the barrel, adjusting the rifle's position until he can see the centre of the target through the centre of the bore. Without moving the rifle, he then looks through the telescopic sight to see where the crosshairs fall, adjusting for windage and elevation until they coincide with the view down the rifle's barrel. The elevation turret on the scope is then adjusted to give the bullet an appropriate trajectory according to the range of the target. For example, a half-minute adjustment moves the strike of the bullet 12mm (0.5in) for each 90m (300ft) of range.

As well as considerations of range, the sniper has to take into account the strength and direction of the wind. As wind velocity increases, the effect on the bullet increases, dependant on its direction and the range of the shot. For the purposes of sniping, the so-called 'clock system' is used to determine the direction from where the wind is blowing and its velocity. Thus, a wind blowing from

Below: A temporary sniper hide in the field. The sniper 'hugs' the earth, his body and weapon heavily camouflaged.

Right: A British Royal Marine sniper in polar terrain. The furniture of his weapon, a 7.62mm Accuracy International PM, is coloured to blend in with the white surroundings.

right to left across the sniper's front is called a three o'clock wind; one blowing at the same angle but left to right is a nine o'clock wind. These two winds have most effect on a bullet, so are called full-value winds.

There are three methods an elite forces sniper can use to evaluate wind speed. The flag method involves the sniper observing flag or cloth hanging from a pole and estimating the angle from the tip of the flag to the mast. In this way he can work out the wind velocity by dividing four (a numerical constant) into the angle in degrees to get wind velocity in miles per hour. There will

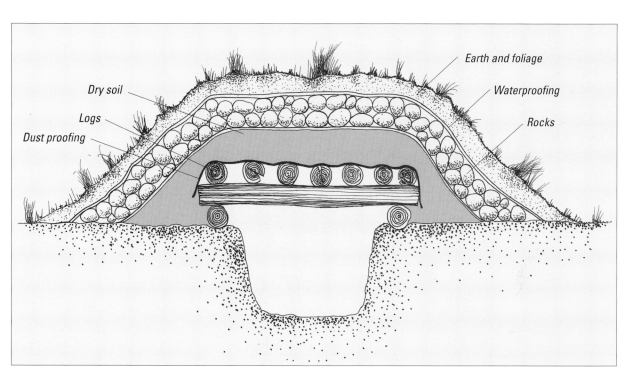

Dry soil

Earth and foliage

Logs

Waterproofing

Dust proofing

Rocks

obviously be few flags on a battlefield, so the second method of estimating wind velocity, the observation method, can be used. Snipers can use observation in the following ways: a wind under 4.8kph (3mph) can hardly be felt, but causes smoke to drift; a 4.8-8kph (3-5mph) wind is felt lightly on the face; an 8-13kph (5-8mph) wind keeps trees in constant motion; a 13-19kph (8-12mph) wind raises dust and loose paper; and a 19-24kph (12-15mph) wind causes small trees to sway. A third way to determine wind velocity is to 'read' the wind by the spotting scope method. The sun heats up the earth's surface, causing heat waves, which appear to ripple and rise straight up from the ground on a calm day. Any movement of air, however slight, will send these waves in the direction of the air flow. By determining whether the waves appear to be slow or fast and from left or right, the sniper will be able to determine wind velocity and wind direction. However, only after constant practice will a sniper become proficient in determining how much windage adjustment to put on his rifle.

After he has determined the wind velocity and direction, the sniper can use the following formula to work out the windage correction: R x V divided by 15 (R is the range in hundreds of yards, V is the wind velocity in miles per hour and 15 is a numerical constant). This formula is accurate up to 457m (1500ft); beyond this it varies due to velocity loss. However, by changing the numerical constant the correct windage can be determined. At 550m (1800ft) the constant becomes 14, at 640-732m (2100-2400ft) 13, at 823m (2700ft) 12 and at 914m (3000ft) 11.

For the hostage-rescue and counter-terrorist sniper, as well as the problems of range and windage, there is the consideration of over-penetration. If a sniper in the field in wartime misses his shot he will not worry where the bullet goes (he will be hoping that it at least hits another enemy soldier), but he will be more concerned if he has been spotted by the enemy. However, for the hostage-rescue sniper it is different. Bullets can travel for hundreds of metres, and can be a danger to innocent civilians. In urban areas, for

Above: Cross section of a field sniper's camouflaged hide showing the materials used in its construction.

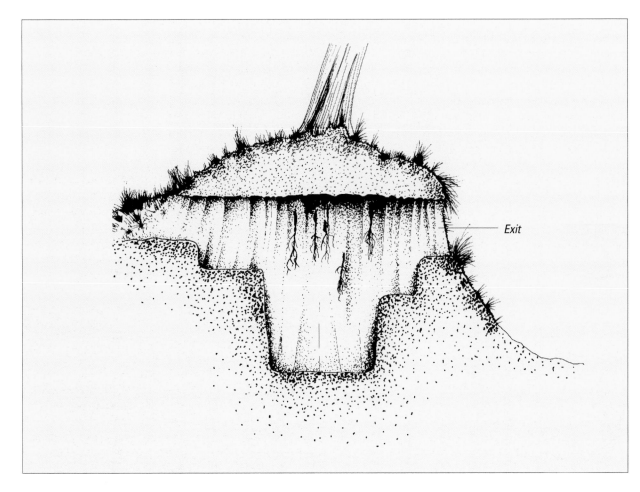

Exit

Above: Cross-section of a sniper's tree hide. Trees which have deep roots are preferred, and a tree at the back of the tree line affords better cover from enemy observation.

example, the sniper must always watch the target's background to estimate the risk of over-travel. A brick wall, for example, may stop a bullet, but if it is merely a plaster partition then a bullet could go through it and injure innocent parties in the next room. For this reason hostage-rescue snipers take up positions on high ground, so that a miss or over-penetration round will strike the ground very close to the target and stop.

The next problem for the sniper is where to aim at on the body. Again the hostage-rescue sniper has fewer choices then his military counterpart because his shot must be instantly incapacitating. In the field, on the other hand, a shot which only wounds is still of benefit, as enemy resources will be tied up evacuating the wounded individual, and an

opponent's overall morale will also be reduced. That said, all snipers want to achieve an instant 'stop', and to do this means hitting a vital organ. Rifle bullets generally cause more severe wounds than handgun bullets because of their much higher velocities. A high-powered rifle round, for example, will travel at a speed of around 900mps (2920fps), whereas a handgun round's velocity is around 350mps (1140fps).

One very important effect of a high-speed rifle round is hydrostatic shock – the pressure wave it produces by displacement of water-carrying tissue. This results in a temporary cavity many times larger than the size of the permanent cavity drilled by the bullet itself. The pressure wave damages tissue in the body far from the wound track and can destroy an organ that the bullet does not hit directly (this explains the serious bullet wounds, which have small entrance and exit holes). Another effect of a bullet is to cause secondary missiles – bone splinters – to shoot into the body. Each one of these creates its own wound track, thus enhancing the destructive force of the round. However, the hostage-rescue sniper has a problem: if a suspect is holding a hostage very close as a shield, a secondary missile can hit the hostage. In such a situation it is best to fire when the suspect is behind the hostage, rather than alongside or in front (there will be normally be more than one sniper deployed, each one having different viewpoints).

A shot in the central nervous system, such as in the spine, will cause the target to drop immediately because it interrupts the nerve impulses that control voluntary movement. A hit high on the spine can also kill by stopping heartbeat and respiration. The brain is the best part of the central nervous system to destroy for an instantaneous stop. The brain itself is composed of several parts: the cerebrum, which controls thought, the cerebellum, which controls muscles, and the medulla oblogata, which controls the heart and lungs. Fortunately for the sniper, a hit anywhere in the brain cavity will destroy the entire brain due to hydrostatic shock. Because of the confined space within the cranial cavity, a bullet penetrating the skull will

Below: A US Marine and his spotter in Saudi Arabia during the 1991 Gulf War. His weapon is the bolt-action 7.62mm M-40A1 rifle.

do great damage to the immediate area. The result is instant loss of consciousness and a stopping of the life functions. A sniper firing at the face of a target will aim anywhere on the centreline of the face to guarantee a hit on the brain or spinal cord. From the side he will aim for the centre of the brain. A shot in the neck will damage the windpipe and major blood vessels, but it will not necessarily be instantaneously disabling. Similarly, a shot to the rear of the head will be aimed at the brain to drop the target at once.

If the range is too great for a head shot, then the sniper will attempt a body shot. In this case he will aim for the centre of the torso to try and hit the vital organs. As well as hitting these organs, a shot to the torso reduces the probability of a miss (at long ranges wind effects are very unpredictable).

In some cases the sniper will be close to the target but the head will not be visible. In this scenario the firer has three areas to shoot at. First, the spine is vulnerable because cutting the spinal cord will paralyse the target instantly (a hit in the lower spine will affect the legs, but not the arms). The second area is the solar plexus, immediately below the rib cage. A bullet which hits this area will result in a severe wound and cause the target to double over. Third, the kidneys are vulnerable because of the nerve complex and the large blood supply. A shot to the kidneys will send the victim into shock, paralysing him until he passes out from loss of blood.

During hostage-rescue operations, police and military snipers will always try for head shots. An excellent example of hostage-rescue snipers in action occurred in February

Below: A sniper's range card. The ranges of terrain features, their required sight settings and where to aim if a target appears at specific points are all marked on the card as shown.

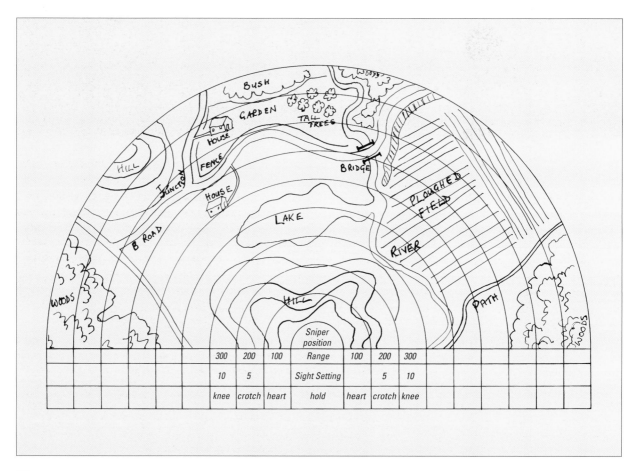

			300	200	100	Range	100	200	300				
			10	5		Sight Setting		5	10				
			knee	crotch	heart	hold	heart	crotch	knee				

1976, when terrorists of the *Front de Libération de la Côte de Somalie* (FLCS) took 28 French schoolchildren, their teacher and a bus driver hostage on a school bus in Djibouti. The French counter-terrorist unit, GIGN, was deployed in case the affair could not be brought to a peaceful conclusion. The terrorists demanded the withdrawal of French troops from the colony of Djibouti, otherwise the hostages would die. The commander of the GIGN men was Lieutenant Christian Prouteau, who observed that the terrorists on the bus, only a few metres away from a Somali border post, were in constant communication with Somali troops (Somalia at that time was ruled by a Marxist government, which was highly supportive of 'liberation movements'). Prouteau had been ordered not to open fire unless there was

only one terrorist on the bus. He had argued with his superiors in Paris to relent on this order; reluctantly they had agreed that he could assault the bus when there were two terrorists on board. But as the afternoon wore on, the minimum number on the bus at any one time remained at three (there were four terrorists in total).

Prouteau had four snipers covering the bus and a further two keeping watch on the two Somali heavy machine guns pointing in their direction. There were also two platoons of French Foreign Legionnaires guarding his outer perimeter. He realised that negotiations were going nowhere and so decided to attack. With three terrorists inside the bus and the fourth outside, he gave his men the order to fire. Bullets from the Gendarmes' 7.62mm FR-F1 sniper rifles smashed into the

Above: Snipers in the field. Note how well they blend into their surroundings, and how they have selected a position with a wide field of view and arc of fire.

heads of all four terrorists. The terrorist outside the bus was hit by four rounds before he crashed to the ground, the one on the back seat was hit three times in the head, the one near the driver's seat was hit twice in the head, as was the one walking down the aisle.

But then the Somali machine guns opened fire on the Frenchmen, as did other Somali troops who had previously been concealed. Prouteau's reserve snipers opened fire and temporarily silenced the two machine guns. When the French Foreign Legion arrived, Prouteau and his men had to make a dash for the bus to rescue the still-stranded schoolchildren. As one of the Gendarmes reached the front door of the bus, another terrorist appeared as from nowhere and raced through the vehicle's back door, opening up with his submachine gun in an attempt to slaughter the hostages. Taking temporary cover, the Gendarme took careful aim with his revolver, then drilled the terrorist's head with three shots. Other Gendarmes rushed on board, smashed the windows with their pistol butts and began passing the children to waiting Foreign Legion jeeps. Tragically, one had died and a further five had been wounded by terrorist fire, but the other 24 were evacuated unharmed. The Somalis lost 28 killed, the majority by sniper fire fire from the GIGN marksmen.

Rescue at Marseilles

Nearly 18 years later, GIGN snipers were again in action, this time on the soil of France herself, and again they displayed their superb shooting skills. On 24 December 1994, Algerian terrorists of the Armed Islamic Group (GIA) seized an Air France A300 Airbus en route from Algeria to Majorca, along with 227 passengers and 12 crew. After releasing some passengers and killing a French embassy staffer and dumping his body on the tarmac, the terrorists ordered the aircraft to be flown to France. Landing at Marseilles airport, the terrorists issued a number of demands, including that the aircraft be refuelled to allow it to fly to

Paris. French officials realised that they intended to crash it into the city, and so the decision was taken to assault the aircraft.

The commander of the GIGN team, Major Denis Favier, deployed his men, placing a sniper team in the airport's control tower. The assault itself was conducted by 25 Gendarmes, and in less than a minute the aircraft was secured and the passengers evacuated. Nearly a dozen had been wounded in the gun battle, along with nine Gendarmes, but at last the terrorists were isolated in the cockpit. The escape of the co-pilot – the last remaining hostage – from the cockpit by jumping onto the tarmac from an open window, gave the snipers in the control tower complete freedom of view. The French snipers opened fire with their FR-F2 sniper rifles fitted with Modèle 53 telescopic sights. All four terrorists were quickly killed inside the cockpit.

Israel's Crack Marksmen

Another unit that puts a significant emphasis on marksmanship is the Israeli National Police Border Guard's *Ya'ma'm* (Special Police Unit). On 7 March 1988, the unit was involved when three Palestinian terrorists seized eight women and one man on a bus near Dimona in the Negev Desert. The bus was surrounded by *Ya'ma'm* negotiators and snipers, but the terrorists murdered one of the hostages. At 1015 hours, therefore, the snipers opened fire and all three terrorists were killed by head shots, though not before they had killed two more hostages. Interestingly, one of the weapons used by Israeli snipers is the Galil sniper rifle. This is a semi-automatic weapon, which allows the sniper to get off two or more rounds in quick succession. On 8 September 1992, for example, an Israeli psychopath who murdered four women in a health clinic in Jerusalem was shot and killed by a *Ya'ma'm* sniper with two shots in succession from a Galil.

The hostage-rescue and counter-terrorist sniper has a disadvantage with regard to his military counterpart when it comes to firing

Opposite page: The French FR-F1 sniper rifle, used by the GIGN team at Djibouti in 1976.

Right: Examples of reticle designs. For the sniper the best are the duplex design (1), which has thick lines at the outside of the field, and the simple crosshair variety (3). The post reticle (2) is also good, though the dot reticle (4) can blot out a good portion of the target.

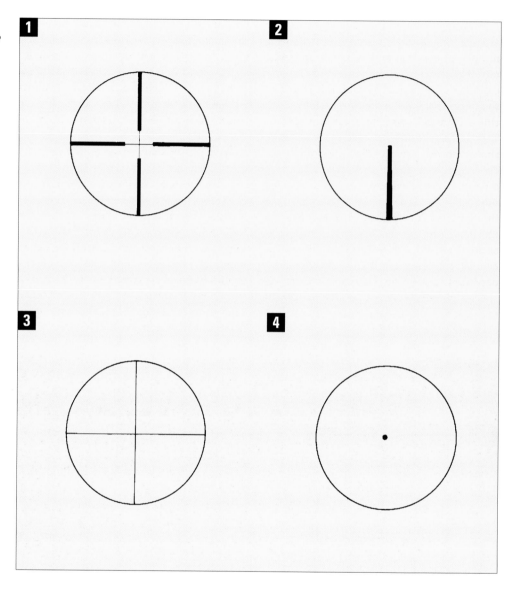

positions. The prone position is best for sniping, but is rare for the police sniper because of obstructions. During a hostage rescue, for example, the sniper is likely to be sitting or in a position between sitting and lying prone.

The prone position offers the lowest silhouette and is ideal, both for cover and for a stable shooting position. For the optimum firing position the sniper must stand facing the target with the left hand well forward and the right hand grasping the stock at the heel of the butt. When lying on the ground the sniper forces the butt of the rifle into his right shoulder, grips the small of the stock with his right hand and lowers his right elbow to the ground so his shoulders are level. The sniper can determine whether he has a good, well balanced shooting position if the sight crosshairs move over the target between six o'clock and 12 o'clock as he breathes. Many sniper rifles now come fitted with bipods, which make for a much more stable firing position. In this case the bipod supports the gun rather than the forearm.

Regardless of the position a sniper assumes for shooting, he has to take in a number of points to ensure his shot is accurate. The shouldering of his weapon is critical because of muzzle jump. If the butt isn't solidly against the shoulder for each shot the rifle will recoil, with the muzzle jumping. This will affect the accuracy of subsequent shots. Similarly, the so-called 'spot weld' (the cheek against the stock) is very important for a consistent sight picture. 'Canting', or tipping the rifle left or right, places the sight to the right or left of the barrel, which has the effect of throwing the impact point to the side and ruins the shot. Canting can be avoided by keeping the butt solidly into the shoulder and maintaining a good 'spot weld'.

Special forces snipers spend hundreds, even thousands, of hours on ranges honing their skills, but these skills will count for little unless they have the right equipment. The actual rifles used for sniping need certain attributes to make them effective tools, and these will be discussed below. Needless to say, no one weapon fulfils every sniper rifle criteria. Nevertheless, there are some rifles which are used throughout the world more than others.

What are the qualities looked for in sniper rifles? Accuracy is important for obvious reasons. In the field a sniper will want a rifle that will, with the sights adjusted accordingly, guarantee a head shot up to a range of at least 300m (975ft) and a body shot up to a range of 1000m (3250ft). The question of range leads on to problems of calibre. Traditionally sniper rifles have been 7.62mm or thereabouts, thus improving the chance of a hit at long range. For hostage-rescue work, however, long-range firepower is not

Below: A Spetsnaz sniper with a Dragunov sniper rifle fitted with the PSO-1 telescopic sight, which can detect infrared emissions. This enables the firer to operate in low-light conditions.

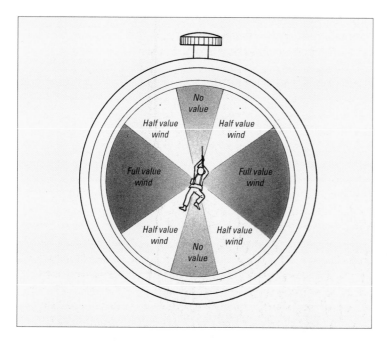

Above: The clock system used by snipers to determine wind direction and velocity. Such information is vital for an accurate shot.

required: engagement ranges are usually around 100m (320ft). For this type of work rifles firing 5.56mm rounds have a number of advantages. They have minimum recoil so it is easier to shoot more accurately, and the lighter rounds are less likely to go through structural materials.

A specialist class of weapon is the so-called 'anti-materiel rifle', a large, heavy rifle firing an extremely powerful cartridge. A good example is the US M82A1, a semi-automatic which is some 1.6m (60in) long and fires the 12.7mm Browning heavy machine gun cartridge. This is accurate out to some 1500m (4900ft) and is effective against vehicles, aircraft on the ground, military equipment and, of course, personnel.

As well as differences in calibre, snipers have a choice of bolt-action and semi-automatic models. In general semi-automatics are reckoned to be inherently less accurate than bolt-action rifles. A semi-automatic has more moving parts and more chances of malfunctions than a bolt-action model. But whatever the rifle, it is imperative that it holds its zero so that the sniper will be able to place his shot where he wants. Wood and other mate-

rials used in the construction of rifle stocks expand with temperature, and wood absorbs moisture, which also causes expansion. If the stock material presses on the barrel it will cause a change in the point of impact. To prevent this it is necessary to have free-floating barrels, where the mount is such that no wood touches the barrel. Some snipers, especially those in police and paramilitary units, require suppressed sniper weapons. A truly suppressed weapon has to be designed as such from the start, normally with a larger diameter tube surrounding the barrel, and containing a system of baffles which absorb the sound of the high-pressure gasses leaving the barrel. A less effective method is the add-on silencer, usually a large-diameter tube screwed onto the end of the barrel. Suppression serves several purposes: it helps the report blend into any background noise, making it possible to shoot suspects without others hearing the shots; it eliminates muzzle flash – important for night missions – and it reduces the recoil of the rifle. But if a high-velocity bullet is used, the supersonic 'crack' of its travel counteracts the effects of suppression at the rifle. For truly silent operation, a less-powerful subsonic round is necessary, implying a shot at relatively close range. But what of ammunition?

Sniper Ammunition

The US Marines Corps' sniping manual states the following concerning sniper rifle ammunition: 'Match quality ammunition will normally be issued because of its greater accuracy and reduced sensitivity to the wind.' For the field sniper, match quality ammunition is the rule not the exception (accuracy is also tied to bullet weight; a heavier bullet can better resist wind deflection: the .308in round offers a good compromise between power, recoil and wind-resisting ability).

Weapons such as the US Marines Corps' M40A sniper rifle and the Green Berets' M24 models are conventional bolt-action designs. However, whereas the M40 has a wooden stock, the M24's is synthetic, made from

Kevlar-graphite, with an aluminium bedding block and adjustable butt plates. Both are 7.62mm calibre, being designed primarily for field use. A more advanced sniper rifle, currently in use with the British SAS and the British Army as a whole, is the Accuracy International PM, designated L96A1 in service use. Designed from the beginning as a military sniping rifle capable of hitting the target with the first shot in any conditions, and with a clean or fouled barrel, the PM has an aluminium frame. The frame itself is clad in a high-impact plastic stock in which the barrel floats freely. The rifle comes equipped with a fully adjustable bipod and a monopod in the butt. This can be lowered and adjusted to allow the sniper to lay his sights on and observe the target without having to support the weight of the rifle for long periods. The sights themselves are Schmidt & Bender 6 x 24, which guarantee a first-round hit up to a range of 600m (1950ft).

Like many sniper rifles, the PM is built in a number of variants. The suppressed version, for example, uses special subsonic ammunition and is accurate up to a range of 300m (975ft). Regarding ammunition, the PM comes in a number of calibres, such as 0.300 Winchester Magnum and 7mm Remington Magnum for targets up to 1000m (3250ft) away. The 0.338 Super Magnum version of the PM uses a times 10 telescopic sight and fires 0.338 Lapua Magnum ammunition. This combination means it can hit targets well beyond a range of 1000m (3250ft), and the round is still supersonic up to a range of 1400m (4550ft). Whereas most sniper rifles have a muzzle velocity of around 750-800mps (2440-2600fps), the Super Magnum's is 914 mps (2970fps).

The Swiss firm SIG-Sauer produces sniper rifles that are in service with police and counter-terrorist units around the world. Its SSG 2000 model, for example, is in use with UK and Far Eastern police forces. A bolt-action rifle, its barrel is equipped with a combination flash suppressor and muzzle brake, which allows for a fast, controlled follow-up

Below: One of the excellent sniper rifles produced by the Swiss firm SIG-Sauer. This is the 5.56mm SG551 rifle. All SIG weapons are superbly engineered, giving the reliability vital for sniper work.

Right: Hostage-rescue snipers need to choose their positions with care to avoid presenting themselves as targets. Here are three examples of the right and wrong positions.

shot. The French FR-F2 sniper rifle has a barrel encased in a thick plastic thermal sleeve. This, claim the manufacturers, reduces the likelihood of heat haze interfering with the line-of-sight, and also reduces the infrared signature of the weapon.

The 7.62mm Galil sniper rifle is specially designed to meet the requirements of the marksman. Like the standard Galil, it is a semi-automatic, gas-operated rifle which has a number of additional features to improve accuracy. The bipod, for example, is mounted behind the fore-end and attached to the receiver so it can be adjusted by the firer. The barrel, which is heavier than standard and thus gives greater accuracy, is fitted with a muzzle brake and compensator, which reduces jump and allows speedy re-alignment of the weapon after firing. Another semi-automatic rifle is the SVD Dragunov, in service with most armies that use Russian or ex-Soviet bloc equipment. Tough and reliable, it fires a nineteenth-century vintage 7.62mm rimmed cartridge.

One weapons manufacturer with a high reputation among the world's counter-terrorist units is Heckler & Koch. The German unit GSG 9, for example, uses the company's 7.62mm PSG 1 sniper rifle. A semi-automatic model, it has superb accuracy. The latter attribute is especially important to hostage-rescue units, as a GSG 9 commander explains: 'The sniper has only one shot and that has to put the terrorist out of action. There's no time for a second shot because the hostage would already be dead.'

Below: Spanish GEO counter-terrorist snipers during training. The anti-terrorist sniper usually has only one chance to kill his target. Such a requirement demands high accuracy from both marksman and his weapon.

CHAPTER 8

AUTOMATIC WEAPONS

Assault rifles and submachine guns are essential to elite teams. More than anything else, it is the weapons skills of special forces soldiers which sets them apart from conventional soldiers and gives them the edge in battle. But small arms proficiency requires thousands of hours of training.

This chapter will examine one of the most important special forces skills: the ability to wield and shoot personal automatic and semi-automatic weapons accurately. The current US Special Forces training manual has an introductory paragraph that could be the weapons philosophy of any elite unit: 'If Special Operations Forces (SOF) are to effectively execute the various missions for which they were designed, they must be prepared to use deadly force. Your ability to use your shooting skills with confidence and without hesitation will help to ensure the success of any mission.'

The shooting skills of elite troops must be considerably higher than those of conventional forces. The chief reason for this is the operational doctrine of crack units. Special forces teams invariably operate in a hostile environment, often far away from friendly lines and on foot. They rely on their camouflage and concealment skills to evade enemy forces, but if they are compromised in any way they have to rely on their weapons skills either to destroy the enemy force or buy enough time to escape. However, because elite troops operate in small-sized teams, such as the British SAS four-man team or US Green Beret 12-man A-Team, they are invariably outnumbered in a firefight. In such a situation each elite soldier has to make every round count. Examples will be given below

Left: Hostage-rescue soldiers practice rapid-entry drills. Fast and accurate shooting in such scenarios is crucial to getting hostages out alive.

Above: Range work is essential for perfecting marksmanship and slick weapons skills. Only countless hours spent training will develop the instinctive shooting techniques demanded of all elite troops.

of special forces teams surviving contacts while outnumbered by up to 20 to one. However, when one compares the weapons philosophy of specialist units to those of conventional forces, such feats will not appear out of the ordinary.

The weapons philosophy of all elite forces is as follows: in the attack, create sufficient shock firepower to break enemy resistance and suppress hostile fire to enable assault elements to close with their targets; in the defence, break up hostile attacks with accurate, long-range firepower before the enemy can bring his firepower to bear. The key word is accurate. Studies have shown that on the twentieth-century battlefield only around 15 per cent of conventional infantrymen fire their weapons, and because of fear, fatigue and stress, those 15 per cent only fire at ranges below 100m (320ft), and then inaccurately. In addition, when ambushed it has been shown that only 10 per cent of infantrymen return fire. Thus any unit which can lay down accurate fire from all its members will stand a good chance of emerging victorious.

Learning such skills takes time, and begins with learning the basic principles of combat marksmanship. American military specialists state that there are eight basic fundamentals of marksmanship.

First, the correct stance is vital for accurate shooting. In the standing position the feet should be shoulder-width apart, with the non-firing foot slightly forward of the firing foot and pointed at the target. The firing foot itself should be positioned to give good balance, as well as to facilitate forward and lateral movement. The knees are slightly bent and the upper torso leans forward. A correct stance necessitates the soldier having 60-70 per cent of his weight forward to absorb the weapon's recoil.

Grip and Alignment

Second, grip is very important for accuracy. When holding a handgun, for example, many elite troops will use the so-called Weaver grip. This shooting position was designed by Los Angeles Country Deputy Sheriff Jack Weaver, hence the name. With the Weaver grip, the forefinger of the left hand is placed in front of the trigger guard for extra support.

Third is sight alignment, which entails centring the front sight blade into the rear sight notch. The top of the front sight must be level with the top of the rear sight and in alignment with the eye. But how does the elite soldier know which is his dominant eye? He extends his arm and points a finger at an object. Next he closes his left eye first and looks at the finger with his right eye. He then reverses the process; whichever eye observes the finger pointing directly at the object is the dominant eye.

Fourth, the sight picture is essential to accurate shooting. This is the positioning of the weapon's sights in relation to the target as seen by the firer when he aims his weapon. A correct sight picture consists of proper sight alignment with the front sight placed at the centre of the target. The human eye can only focus on one object at a time at different distances; the final focus of the eye is always on the front sight.

Breathing is also very important. The special forces soldier is taught to breathe properly to achieve accuracy. The sequence is as follows: take a breath, let it out, then inhale normally; exhale a little air until comfortable, hold and then fire.

Trigger Control and Recovery

The sixth aspect is trigger control. When firing, the slack of the trigger must be removed, then a steady increase in pressure must be applied towards the rear without interruption or snatching.

Seventh, follow-through entails the shooter maintaining concentration after firing. In this way he will not disturb sight alignment.

Recovery, the eighth point, is the return of the weapon to the original holding position in the centre of the aiming area, with a natural sight alignment. The use of the correct stance and grip ensures a smooth recovery.

Shooting a weapon on a range and carrying it ready for use on operations are two very different things. Therefore, elite troops are taught ready positions for holding their weapons. An M16 assault rifle, for example, can be carried in the low ready position to facilitate speedy firing. The stock of the rifle is placed firmly in the firing shoulder, with the muzzle pointed downwards at a 45-degree angle. When it has to be fired, it is simply raised up to the line of sight.

There will be occasions, especially during anti-ambush drills, when the elite soldier has no time for slow, aimed fire. In this situation he will employ a method of shooting known as the aimed quick kill. If shooting a rifle, he will not look through his rear sight but look over it to focus on the front sight. The top of the front sight is placed slightly below the desired point of impact on the target. This method is fine for shooting at targets up to a

Above: The spearhead formation, an ideal elite unit tactic for moving across open country. Maximum firepower can be brought to bear both front and flanks in a matter of seconds.

range of 12m (40ft). Rapid aimed fire is another excellent firing technique for hitting targets at 15m (50ft) or less. At such ranges there is no time to ensure a correct sight picture. Therefore, rapid aimed fire is a compromise between a proper sight picture and aimed quick kill. As the weapon is raised to eye level, the point of focus switches from the target to the front sight, while the firer ensures that the front and rear sights are in alignment left and right.

When the elite soldier has mastered the above techniques he will then learn the 'double tap'. This is one of the most difficult engagement techniques to perform correctly; it is two shots fired from a weapon in quick succession. However, that is a great simplification. The idea is to place two sighted rounds in the kill zone as quickly as possible, not to fire off two rounds in the hope that one will hit. There are two reasons for employing the double tap. First, two rounds

increase the probability of a kill. Second, no matter how well a firer shoots, there is always a chance that he will miss with only one round.

All the above techniques take a great deal of time to perfect, Just a casual glance at the range work performed by the world's leading elite units emphasises the point. Each French GIGN gendarme will fire 9000 rounds on the range with his pistol each year and 3000 rounds with his rifle. With his revolver, he must be able to hit a moving target at a range of 25m (80ft) or more in two seconds. In addition, he must also show that he can hit a 'vital' spot on six targets at a range of 25m (80ft) in less than five seconds. This means that each GIGN member must spend at least two hours on the range every day to maintain his ability to shoot fast and accurately. Fast, accurate fire translates into being able to run with a rifle, align the sights and open fire on the target within two seconds of reaching the firing point. A target score of 98 out of 100 at a range of 200m (650ft), with or without telescopic sights, is considered normal. Submachine guns and hostage-rescue weapon drills will be discussed below, but mention should be made of the time each US Delta Force team member spends on the ranges during his career. He will spend 15-20 hours each week on the range, firing an estimated 3000 rounds per week from his MP5 submachine gun.

One of the reasons why special forces soldiers perform so well in battle is that the drills they learn in training are so well rehearsed and ingrained that they become second nature. This is not to say that they do not experience human emotions during the white-hot intensity of combat. The British SAS eight-man patrol codenamed 'Bravo Two Zero' operated behind Iraqi lines during the 1991 Gulf War. After being inserted its position was discovered by the enemy, provoking

Below: Members of the Los Angeles Special Weapons and Tactics (SWAT) Team practise pistol shooting. The correct sight alignment, stance and trigger control are essential when the firer has to kill with his first shot.

an assault by Iraqi armour and infantry. The SAS commander, Sergeant Andy McNab, relates his emotions as the battle began: 'In the British Army you are taught how to react when the enemy opens fire: you dash to make yourself a hard target, you get down, you crawl into a fire position, find the enemy, set your sights at the range and fire. "Reaction to Effective Enemy Fire", it's called. That all goes to rat shit when you're actually under fire ... Your instincts compel you to get down and make yourself as small as possible and wait for it all to end ... The emotional side [of the brain] is saying, sod that, stay there, maybe it'll all go away. But you know it's not going to and that something has to be done.'

It is the ability of special forces troops to 'get something done' that enables them to defeat often impossible odds, to close with and defeat the enemy. McNab's team launched an assault against the Iraqis attacking them, undeterred by the odds. McNab again: 'It's no good just lying there and hoping that they won't see you or go away, because they won't ... It takes maximum firepower, balanced with ammunition conservation, to win a firefight. It's a question of you getting more rounds down than them and killing more of them initially, so they either back off or dig their own little holes.'

M16 Requirements

One of the most important aspects of using small arms is making sure each weapon is properly maintained. Though military firearms are designed and built to work in adverse weather conditions, they are still vulnerable to fouling after firing many rounds, or as a result of being immersed in sand, mud and water. A case in point is the M16 assault rifle. It was originally sold as a self-cleaning weapon, until American soldiers in Vietnam discovered that the powder used in the weapon's 5.56mm ammunition contained too much calcium carbonate, which meant the gas tubes soon became clogged, causing a malfunction. A change in the composition

of the propellant and clear instructions as to the gun's cleaning soon rectified the problem. American elite troops fighting in Vietnam and SAS soldiers in Borneo in the 1960s soon discovered another problem with the M16: it retained water in the small diameter bore after being dunked in water or exposed to rainfall. This necessitated pointing the muzzle down, drawing back the cocking handle slightly and, while holding it back, shaking out the water. Drawing back the bolt pulls the cartridge out of the chamber and breaks the seal at that point, which would otherwise stop the water running out.

Weapons Maintenance

Elite troops are taught the importance of proper weapons care and maintenance. This includes cleaning all metal surfaces with nitro solvent, and regularly stripping and cleaning the bolt carrier group. Special attention is paid to making sure the bolt locking lugs, the extractor and the extractor well are all free of dirt and carbon fouling, to stop locking and round extraction problems. A patch of cloth and solvent is used to clean the inside of the receiver, while a small brush can be used to clean around the trigger group; a pipe cleaner is helpful for getting into any tight spaces. The bore and chamber are cleaned with a brush and solvent, while a cord is used to pull an oil-soaked patch of cloth through the barrel. A light coat of oil is also usually applied to the chamber, firing pin and all metal surfaces of the weapon. In general, more lubrication is put on the exterior of the bolt carrier, the external surface of the bolt assembly (apart from the bolt face and locking lugs), the interiors of the upper and lower receiver and its components.

Every piece of the gas system – piston, plug and spring – is carefully cleaned to remove all traces of fouling, usually with a lightly oiled cloth. In dry, sandy conditions, this fresh oil may be left off, as it can attract dust and eventually jam the mechanism. In extreme cold, the weapon may also be left dry to prevent it from freezing up. Magazines

can be a cause of stoppages, so they are stripped down at regular intervals to remove any dirt that has accumulated. Magazines that have been full for some time will be unloaded to save degeneration of the spring.

Even the best maintained weapons will sometimes jam, so elite soldiers must know how to deal with stoppages. The first thing they will do if the weapon stops firing in battle is take cover, then cock it, hook the bolt holding device to lock the bolt open, and then look inside to determine the nature of the stoppage. This drill is known as 'cock, hook and look'. If there are rounds in the magazine but the chamber is empty, this may indicate a gas stoppage, usually caused

Above: US troops in Vietnam. In general they fired 400,000 rounds for each kill. Saturation fire is not an option for elite soldiers with limited supplies of rounds.

Above: In the field, elite soldiers have to conserve their ammunition. Any bursts are short and controlled, and aimed fire is the rule.

by dirt or fouling. In this case the cocking handle is pulled back to chamber the next round. If the weapon refuses to load again, then the working parts are released and the gas regulator can be turned to increase the pressure. Failure to fire may also be due to feeding difficulties. If a round is half-fed out of the magazine or there are two rounds jammed on the feedway, this is called a feedway stoppage. In this situation the firer has either to try and shake the loose round out or

remove the magazine and extract the round that way. Feedway stoppages are often the result of insufficient gas to complete the loading and extraction cycle, a symptom of damaged magazines, or of failure to push the rounds right to the back of the magazine during filling.

Having a well maintained personal weapon and knowing how to deal with any stoppages are crucial to special forces' weapons skills, but so are combat shooting techniques. As stated above, there is a big difference between shooting at targets on a range and shooting enemy soldiers in battle, but elite troops must bridge this gap if they are to perform well in combat. Most units adhere to the British SAS's dictum: train hard, fight easy. This means trying to create a training environment that resembles a battlefield, and using live rounds, smoke and all the sounds that pertain to modern warfare. In this way soldiers will not be surprised when they encounter a real battlefield, because they will have already experienced its sights, sounds and dangers (men are occasionally killed or injured in realistic battlefield training scenarios).

Firing Techniques

One of the first things they will be taught is that there are three types of fire used in combat: deliberate, snapshooting and rapid fire. Deliberate fire is used for firing at ground features where the enemy is known to be located, and for enemy positions visible only as muzzle flashes. Deliberate fire is the only really sensible way of engaging targets at long ranges. The rate of deliberate fire is about five rounds per minute, with the firer shooting from a proper firing position and having a clear sight picture. Snapshooting is similar to deliberate fire, but the firer must speed up his actions and reduce the time between shots. It is used against targets which expose themselves at irregular intervals for only a few seconds. For such shooting the firer carries his weapon in the alert position, i.e. butt in the shoulder and finger resting on the trigger. As soon as a target appears the firer can restrain his breathing, take aim and fire quickly and accurately, with attention being paid to not snatching at the trigger. Firing is continued until the target falls or goes back into cover.

Rapid fire involves firing a quick succession of rounds. Similar to snapshooting, it is conducted at a faster pace and more rounds are fired – up to 20 accurate rounds a minute is possible. The most important thing is to

maintain a rhythm, which will enable a firer to restrain his breath, get a clear sight of the target, fire a shot and follow it through in the correct sequence.

Hitting a moving target also involves remembering that it will continue to move during the time it takes for the bullet to hit it. To compensate for this the firer has to aim in

Below: The arcs of fire of a special forces four-man patrol moving in file. Rapid-reaction drills allow the team to direct firepower in any direction.

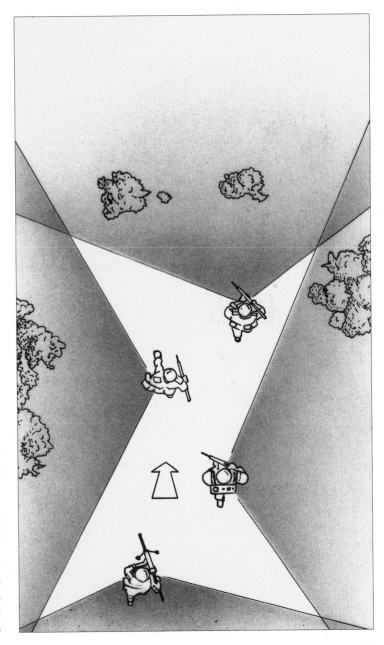

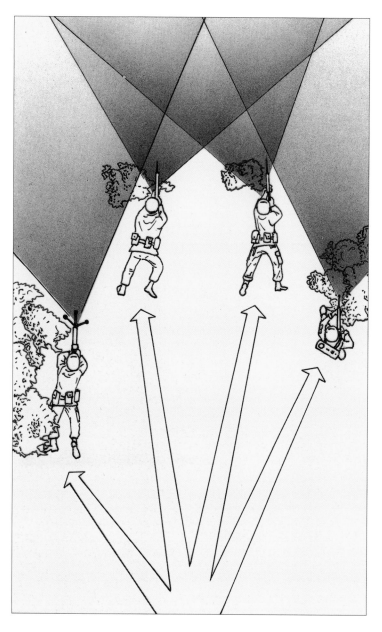

Above: The head-on contact drill of a special forces four-man patrol. In a contact to the front, team members advance right and left of the point man to bring their weapons to bear.

ideal, but for use in the field (unless at close ranges) it will not give a rifle firer any advantage over aimed, semi-automatic fire. And the expenditure of ammunition can be ferocious. For example, during World War I each American soldier fired around 7000 rounds for each enemy casualty; this increased to 25,000 during World War II; 50,000 rounds during the Korean War; and in Vietnam, when the infantry was armed with a weapon capable of full-automatic fire – the M16 – the rate had increased to a staggering 200,000-400,000 rounds for each enemy soldier killed. Full-automatic fire tends to pull the weapon up and to the right as the cartridge cases are ejected, which disturbs the aim picture and causes all except the first two or three rounds to strike off target. The M16A2 and many other modern semi-automatic rifles are capable of three-round bursts, which offer a good compromise and can be used for enemy suppression if suddenly coming under fire.

SAS Firepower

Andy McNab gives an excellent example of controlled SAS firing techniques during his team's aforementioned contact with the Iraqis: 'Everybody was getting the rounds down. The Minimis were fired in bursts of 3-5 rounds. Ammunition had to be managed ... You don't fire on the move. It slows you up. All you have to do is get forward, get down and get firing so that the others can move up. As soon as you get down on the ground your lungs are heaving and your torso is moving up and down, you're looking around for the enemy but you've got sweat in your eyes ... You want to get down in a nice firing position like you do on the range, but it isn't happening that way. You're trying to calm yourself down to see what you're doing, but you want to do everything at once. You want to stop this heavy breathing so you can hold the weapon properly and bring it to bear.'

Of prime importance to elite troops in a firefight, as McNab alludes to, is getting into a firing position that has some sort of cover. When in cover the elite soldier has to

front of the target (known as 'leading' the target) to avoid the shot impacting behind it. The degree of lead will obviously depend on the speed, direction and range of the target's movement, and the farther away the target the greater the amount of lead necessary to compensate for movement.

What about full-automatic fire? For hostage-rescue and similar missions it is remember several rules to maximise his effectiveness. These include trying to rest the forearm to increase accuracy. In addition, the barrel should not be rested on any cover because this will affect its resonance and cause rounds to be displaced. A good firing position from cover is one that offers protection from enemy fire but allows the firer a clear view and wide arc of fire, as well as plenty of room for movement.

When firing from a trench or ditch the elite soldier will choose the right-hand corner to fire from (if he is right-handed; if not, then the left side). Both elbows are placed on the area that forms a shelf at the top of the trench and the base of the cover. The fore-arms are placed on the cover. The cover itself should be earth or sand to absorb enemy rounds – rocks can fragment when hit by bullets, sending sharp splinters into the firer's face. When firing from low banks and folds in the ground the firer must keep his muzzle clearance as close to the top of the bank or crest as possible to ensure maximum concealment. On the other hand, the barrel itself should be clear of the ground when firing, otherwise muzzle blast will kick up a cloud of dust that will be a clear sign of identification to the enemy.

Walls and buildings can offer good concealment but not necessarily good cover. Most modern buildings have walls that are

Below: British SAS soldiers test-fire their M16s prior to a mission in Borneo in the 1960s. Though it requires careful maintenance, the M16 is an excellent assault rifle.

not as thick as older constructions, and a depth of only one brick will not offer much protection against a high-velocity round. The best tactic when firing from walls or buildings is to remove a few bricks and fire through a hole in the wall.

When put into practice, special forces shooting techniques are highly effective. Two examples from the 1991 Gulf War shows how highly trained marksmen can defeat large numbers of conventional soldiers. In February 1991, an eight-man American Special Forces A-Team was inserted into Iraqi territory near the village of Swayjghazi to keep watch for signs of Iraqi troop movements near Baghdad. The Americans constructed two concealed hides in a shallow drainage canal 280m (900ft) west of Highway 7. Discovered by a number of Iraqi children from a nearby village, they fell back along a drainage ditch for 370m (1200ft) and established a defensive perimeter.

Firing Techniques in Action

Alerted by the villagers to the Americans' presence, some 150 Iraqi troops from the local garrison were soon on the scene. Veterans of the prior eight-year war with Iran, they soon began directing a large amount of fire against the Green Berets. The latter, after destroying classified communications equipment, then retreated east to a new fighting position. Having radioed for aerial evacuation and air support, the Green Berets started firing single aimed shots at their attackers. Minutes later US Air Force F-16s swooped down and hit the Iraqis with cluster bombs, while the Green Berets' small-arms fire increased the slaughter. Evacuated by two Black Hawk helicopters, the A-Team suffered no losses, while over 100 Iraqis lay dead on the ground.

A more spectacular example of elite firepower was provided by another group of American Special Forces on 23 February 1991 near the village of Oawan al Hamzah. A three-man Special Forces team were attacked by a large number of Iraqi troops. In a superb feat of marksmanship, one of the team, Sergeant First Class Ronald Torbett, shot and killed an enemy soldier at a range of 830m (2700ft) with his sniper-scoped M16. The three Americans, though, had only 300 rounds between them. Using automatic fire only when they were threatened with being overrun, they held back the Iraqis in a firefight which lasted for nearly two hours before being evacuated under fire by helicopter. The Green Berets suffered no casualties. Such feats are no accident. They are the culmination of hundreds of hours spent on ranges and on exercise practising marksmanship and shooting techniques.

The best troops also need good rifles. One of the most popular assault rifles currently in service is the American M16 and its variants. The reasons why assault rifles are popular among elite troops are not hard to find: light, short weapons equipped with muzzle brakes make for ease of handling, while large-capacity magazines give the firer the option of sustained fire, and properly designed pistol grips and foregrips make hip and shoulder firing possible. The M16 has all of these things, and its designer, Eugene Stoner, incorporated a number of attributes from foreign weapons, such as the straight-line stock, buffer system in the stock, plastic handguard, the carrying handle as part of the receiver, the rear sight mounted on this handle and gas fed through a tube directly onto the bolt carrier.

Assault Rifles

The M16 was used by US elite troops in countless engagements against the enemy in Vietnam. It was certainly not a faultless weapon, as mentioned above, but its advantages far outweighed its bad points.

Other assault rifles popular with elite units around the world include the Austrian Steyr AUG, a 5.56mm bullpup design which is capable of semi-, full-automatic or three-round burst fire. It has excellent accuracy and reliability, and its composite furniture allows it to take a lot of punishment. Russia's Spetsnaz use the 5.45mm AK-74 assault rifle,

which has the famous AK-47 as its ancestor. As such, it has inherited all the attributes of its predecessor, i.e. simplicity and robustness. The AK-74 also has an excellent muzzle brake, which allows burst fire without the muzzle moving away from the line of sight. This, combined with the lower recoil because of the smaller round, makes it a very accurate weapon at short and medium ranges.

In the field elite soldiers put a premium on saving ammunition with careful aimed fire, but for hostage-rescue operations the weapons philosophy is very different. Hostage-rescue and close-quarter combat in general require a different type of weapon, one that can accommodate the principles of

combat in confined spaces. These principles are surprise, speed and violence of action. The US Special Forces close-quarter combat manual states the following about the latter: 'Violence of action can be described as a sudden and explosive force that eliminates the threat with the least chance of compromise. When this is coupled with speed, it enables the assault team members to maintain their element of surprise, thereby preventing the opponent from delivering any coordinated or planned reaction.'

The submachine gun is ideally suited to this type of work. Firing pistol-calibre ammunition and having automatic or selective-fire capabilities, submachine guns can be fired

Above: Weapons maintenance is a chore, but for elite soldiers is essential to ensure their weapons work first time every time.

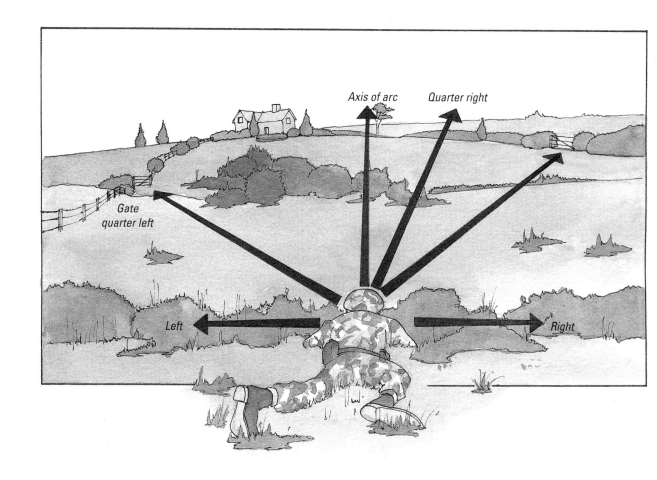

Axis of arc

Quarter right

*Gate
quarter left*

Left

Right

Above: A simple method for elite team members to pinpoint targets to their comrades in the field.

from the shoulder or the hip. For close-quarter work, where the action is usually over in seconds, the submachine gun can be wielded effectively in confined spaces and can put down a large amount of firepower – theoretically between 800 and 1000 rounds per minute – to neutralise any opponent. Submachine gun ammunition has a lower velocity than rifle rounds – around 400mps (1300fps) compared to the M16's 990mps (3200fps) – which means the rounds have less hitting power than rifle rounds, though because of the short ranges they can still go through bodies and hit hostages.

Hostage-rescue units devote hundreds of hours of training to drills for entering build-

ings, railway carriages and aircraft to rescue hostages from armed terrorists. Most of these units have specially-designed ranges that can recreate the scenarios the unit might have to face. The British SAS, for example, has its 'Killing House' at its UK base in Hereford, while the US Delta Force has a similar building called the 'House of Horrors'. Inside these buildings the hostage-rescue teams are put through their paces. When a team clears a room, stun grenades will usually be thrown in first to disorientate the terrorists, then the team members will enter. The latter will be armed with submachine guns, and semi-automatic handguns for back-up weapons (if a team member has a problem with his submachine gun, the standard procedure is to drop down on one knee and draw his handgun, while the man behind him will stand over him until the problem has been rectified). In such an action, the first four seconds are crucial for success. It is therefore imperative that individual team members adopt a good firing stance.

Instructors impress upon their charges that keeping one's balance is vital in close-quarter combat. The body must become a stable weapons platform from which to fire from. Individuals must look just over the sights in the direction of the threat. If possible, submachine guns should be fired from the shoulder with the stock extended, but when clearing rooms elite troops will use the underarm assault position. Used only for work under 10m (30ft), the underarm assault position is the best compromise between speed and accuracy. The butt is placed just inside the armpit, with both elbows held tight against the body. The firer adopts a stable stance and leans forward slightly with the

Below: Three versions of the rugged and reliable Steyr AUG: the standard rifle version (top), the carbine (middle) and the submachine gun (bottom).

Above: Members of the Washington Police Emergency Response Team during hostage-rescue training. Note the M4 rifle being fired from the shoulder. Normally the underarm assault position is used.

feet one pace apart. The firer pushes forward with his right, controlling hand, while pulling back with his left, and his shooting eye is positioned directly over the axis of the barrel. Because there is a tendency to shoot high when using this position the firer aims low, watching where the bullets strike and adjusting fire accordingly.

In addition to being able to fire to the front, elite troops must be able to respond by reflexive action to a target, which appears either to the left or right. This is achieved by the firer swivelling his hips and twisting his torso. In addition, he slightly pivots on his feet, though the feet do not change position

until after his first burst of fire. The movement must be smooth and fluid, with the upper body twisting, the legs flexing, the arms hugging the body and the weapon being thrust forward. If the left foot is forward while a response to the left is made, the left foot stays in position while the right foot is pivoted slightly on the ball of the foot while the right knee is bent slightly. If a response has to be made to the right with the left foot forward, the firer pivots on the balls of both feet.

This snap response, as taught to elite troops, allows the firer to make an instantaneous reaction to danger over an arc of 200 degrees, i.e. 100 degrees on either side of his line of advance. When firing to the left, for example, the stock of the submachine gun swings slightly away from the ribs as the right arm moves away from the body because of the thrusting forward of the right shoulder. Firing to the right is easier but more straining on the torso. The right arm squeezes the stock tight and the left is stretched and tensed to support the weapon. Because the left leg is bent during the whole movement the firer's body will have dropped. This is compensated for by bringing the left hand up slightly while pushing down and thrusting forward with the right.

The other tactics taught to elite troops using submachine guns include keeping away from corners as they drastically reduce

Below: Firing positions for use in urban combat. They involve making use of the best cover available and presenting as small a target as possible to the enemy.

a firer's response time. Though close-quarter combat is conducted at short distances, firers are taught not to get too close to targets for fear of being stabbed by a knife – the greater the distance between firer and his target the more time he has to fire an aimed shot.

Accurate shooting with a submachine gun is made easier by the target identification aids used by hostage-rescue units. These include small but powerful light units, which are mounted underneath the weapon's barrel. Alternatively, a laser aiming dot system puts a red dot onto the target at the point where the bullet will strike, though it does not illuminate the target. However, it greatly aids accuracy when using the under-arm assault position. One of the most powerful currently available, the LEI-100 laser sight, has a range of 600m (1950ft).

The Heckler & Koch MP5

When storming a building to free hostages, hostage-rescue units will usually employ bursts of automatic fire to clear rooms. With most submachine guns an accurate first shot can be difficult because there is a time delay in the operation due to their open-bolt mechanism. The trigger releases the sear, which allows the cocked bolt to move forward, collect a round from the magazine, chamber it and fire it as the bolt closes. However, with the Heckler & Koch MP5 range of submachine guns this is not a problem.

Without doubt the MP5 is the most popular submachine gun for hostage-rescue work. This is because it fires from a closed bolt. Firing from an open bolt means the bolt flies forward to chamber a round when the trigger is pulled, thus resulting in a shift in the weapon's balance. However, the MP5 starts with the bolt closed; when the trigger is pulled all that happens is that the hammer is released to fire the cartridge. There is no shift in the gun's balance and the shot hits where it is aimed. As well as its accuracy, the MP5 is very well engineered, which means it rarely jams – a crucial attribute for a hostage-rescue weapon. There is a shortened MP5K

variant which can be concealed in a bag or under a jacket, while the silenced MP5SD series is useful for killing a sentry or terrorist without alerting his or her comrades.

'Killing House' Tests

A typical SAS 'Killing House' test with the MP5 emphasises the need for the weapon to be accurate with its first shot. The elite soldier walks down a long, dark alley. Suddenly, a door opens and he swings around to see an image of a woman holding a baby. He holds his fire. The door slams shut and he carries on; two seconds later another door opens to reveal the figures of two men holding submachine guns. In less than a second the soldiers hits each target with double taps. As he continues down the alley, another door snaps open to reveal an armed terrorist holding a hostage. Again the soldier hits the target with aimed fire. This ordeal goes on for 45 minutes, with the student's reflexes and marksmanship being tested to the full.

There are some problems associated with submachine guns, though, especially the more compact ones such as the Israeli Uzi and American Ingram. The latter have a lack of left-hand gripping room. The Uzi, for example, has a short foregrip, which has a tendency to slide away from the firer unless he concentrates. Because the foregrips of such weapons do not fill the hand properly they cause the firer to slide his fingers towards the rear. But this means one or two of the firer's fingers might cover the magazine ejection port and cause a stoppage. If, on the other hand, the firer slides his left hand forward, he can get his index finger in front of the barrel, which can result on the end being shot off! At the very least the firer will burn his finger by touching the length of barrel that protrudes from the barrel locking nut. However, these are really minor points, and for the counter-terrorist soldier the submachine gun is the only close-quarter weapon which combines firepower, compactness and lethality. In the hands of a special forces soldier, it is deadly accurate.

Opposite page: An MP5K fitted with a laser aiming system, which puts a red dot onto the target where the bullet is going to strike. Such sights are used by elite teams for hostage-rescue missions.

CHAPTER 9

HEAVY FIREPOWER

Machine guns and mortars provide special forces with increased firepower on the battlefield. In the attack these weapons are substantial force multipliers, while their use and correct deployment in defence allows small-sized teams to beat off attacks against overwhelming odds.

This chapter will examine how elite troops employ machine guns and mortars in attack and defence. The machine gun is an integral part of special forces weapons philosophy. Being primarily a fire support weapon, it is ideally suited to laying down fire across specific areas to prevent enemy movement. In the attack, machine guns can be used to provide support for tactical movement and for general destructive firepower, while in the defence, their range of up to 2000m (6500ft) and beyond gives a small-sized team the opportunity to break up larger enemy formations before they get too close.

In recent years a number of light machine guns have entered service with many armies around the world, giving the elite formations of those armies an opportunity to use easily portable firepower. In the US Army, for example, the introduction into service of the Belgian-designed 5.56mm M249 Squad Automatic Weapon (SAW) has allowed Special Forces, SEALs and Rangers to employ it on offensive operations in preference to the larger calibre and heavier 7.62mm M60 – the latter weighs 10.6kg (23.4lb) as opposed to the SAW's 6.8kg (15lb) – with a corresponding weight saving for the smaller-calibre ammunition. During the 1991 Gulf War, for example, British SAS foot patrols were armed with SAWs (called Minimis in British and Belgian service) in preference to the

Left: The American M60 machine gun, seen here in action in Vietnam. It was used extensively by US Green Beret teams during the Vietnam War.

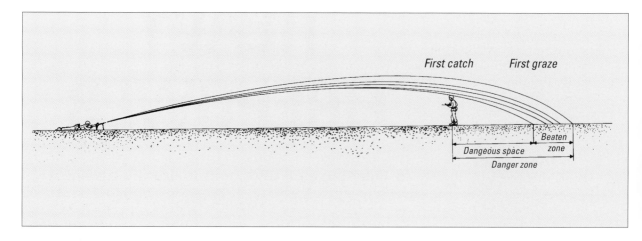

First catch   First graze

Beaten zone

Dangerous space

Danger zone

Above: A machine gun's beaten zone, which is deeper than it is wide. The dangerous space is the area between where the rounds are low enough to hit the top of the target and the point at which they first hit the ground.

weightier 7.62mm General Purpose Machine Guns (GPMGs). The advantage with the SAW is that it can be used like a rifle, being fed from a 200-round plastic belt box (it can also use M16 magazines if required). Another 5.56mm SAW is the Singaporean Ultimax, a lightweight weapon, which feeds from a 100-round drum.

The standard rate of fire for the machine guns of conventional units is 6-20 rounds in each burst. For elite units, even when attacking, this rate falls to 3-5 rounds per burst. The reason is obvious: weapons that have a cyclic rate of fire of up to 1000 rounds per minute have to be strictly controlled to conserve ammunition. There is no doubt that a section armed with one or more machine guns has a large amount of immediate firepower available, but there are certain hard rules with regard to using it that have to be obeyed if the weapon is to perform to its maximum efficiency.

The cyclic rate of fire for the World War II German MG42 machine gun was a staggering 1200 rounds per minute. However, the cyclical rate of fire for a machine gun differs widely from its usable rate of fire. The maximum usable rate of fire is about 250 rounds per minute. If any more shots than this are fired, the barrel of the gun gets so hot that it softens and the weapon loses its accuracy. Therefore, firing is done in bursts, with the firer pausing after each burst to check his

aim or shoot at other targets as required (a loss of accuracy can be disastrous – it is reckoned that the fire effect of a single heavy machine gun is equivalent to that of around 12 assault rifles). The heavy machine gun, because of its heavy mechanical construction, tends to be more capable of maintaining a high rate of fire over long periods. And most belt-fed weapons have quick-change barrels, allowing the firing team to swap the hot barrel for a cool one after a few hundred rounds fired.

An example of the sort of firepower a machine gun is capable of is provided by the exploits of Private First Class Carlos Lozada during the Vietnam War. Lozada was an M60 gunner with the 173rd Airborne Division when in action against North Vietnamese Army (NVA) regulars near Dak To in the Central Highlands on 20 November 1967. He and two other comrades were in a position 350m (1140ft) from their company perimeter and adjacent to Hill 875. Their task was to warn of any enemy approach. As the rest of Lozada's battalion started to advance up Hill 875 they came under fire from enemy trenches. As the battle was raging, an NVA company began to move along a trail near Lozada's outpost. He gave the alarm and then began firing his M60, mowing down 20 NVA troops and stalling their advance. But then he and the rest of his company came under NVA gunfire, which wounded his two comrades.

Lozada and his comrades were ordered to pull back into the battalion perimeter. However, while the two wounded men were being evacuated, Lozada himself continued firing, breaking up another NVA attack. But now he was isolated and being attacked on three sides. He continued to fire, cutting down dozens of NVA with his M60. He was eventually killed, but he had killed scores of the enemy with well aimed, burst fire. For his actions that day Lozada was awarded the Medal of Honor.

Modern medium machine guns are light enough to be manhandled in an assault alongside troops armed with assault rifles. In Vietnam, for example, an M60 gunner would rig nylon webbing across his shoulders to take the weight of the weapon, and would lean forward when firing, holding the muzzle down with his left hand and forearm. With the barrel protruding out in front of him, he could adjust his fire very accurately by observing where his burst hit the enemy. The assistant gunner kept alongside him, feeding the 7.62mm link ammunition into the receiver. That said, the stress and strain on the gunner is considerable. As well as the stress of combat, an M60 gunner carries a load of 36kg (80lb) and the assistant carries an equivalent amount in spare ammunition.

A well sited machine gun in the hands of an experienced gunner can cut an enemy infantry attack to ribbons in seconds, as illustrated above, and in static defence machine

Below: The M60's barrel is lined with stellite, a non-ferrous material which increases the weapon's lifespan. The gun itself is light enough to be fired from the hip – just.

guns are often mounted on tripods. This is particularly desirable when the machine gun is being employed against ground targets. Both accuracy and close grouping of shots can be achieved at long ranges, allowing the machine gun to be used effectively against targets which are well beyond rifle range.

Machine gun fire has a small dispersion and a rather flat trajectory which gives a narrow, dense cone of fire. This results in a long, narrow so-called beaten zone (the area struck by the bullets). In firing over level ground at a range of 750m (2400ft), for example, the height of the cone above ground does not exceed the height of a man. As the range increases the trajectory becomes higher so that fire over obstacles, such as hills and buildings, by indirect laying can be used. A skilled gunner can even fire over the heads of friendly troops. However, the small dispersion of the cone of fire means ranges must be accurately determined. At longer ranges, for example, only a slight error in

range or direction will throw the beaten zone off the target. Machine gunners must therefore be highly trained in estimating ranges.

The French Foreign Legion's combat manual states the following concerning the morale and physical effects of heavy machine-gun fire: 'The morale and physical effects of heavy machine-gun fire are greatest when the fire is delivered with volume at close range, and with the surprise effect from a flank. The physical effect can often be increased by anticipating the probable actions of the enemy after the opening of fire. For example, if fire is placed on an enemy group near cover, such as the edge of a jungle, it is to be expected that the enemy will seek this cover. If the machine gunner foresees the jungle, he will get still more of the enemy as they attempt to gain cover. The morale effect of the fire is greatest when it causes great losses in a short space of time, or is so accurate and heavy as to make the enemy think of little else.'

Below: A typical machine-gun post. The weapon is mounted on a tripod for sustained fire and well entrenched. Ideally, the guns should be positioned to provide all-round fire.

The manual also might have mentioned that the machine gun in a defensive position can also be fired when the gunner's vision is obscured. The GPMG, for example, when tripod mounted, can have a dial sight fitted to the left-hand side of the weapon, which is used when correct aim with the iron sights is not possible. The gunner will have already recorded his lines of fire when visibility was good. When the area is obscured by darkness, fog or smoke, he dials up the coordinates he has recorded on the dial sight, then simply fires blind.

Sighting machine guns is crucial to a successful defence. Ideally, an elite force's commander will place his machine guns to ensure that the enemy will encounter heavy machine gun fire throughout the width and depth of the defended area. This was certainly achieved with the US Special Forces camps constructed in Vietnam (see below). Two rules should always be observed when placing machine guns. First, the guns should be placed in defilade, i.e. hidden from view from the front, to avoid frontal fire. Firing at enemy troops advancing in line from a flank means the machine gun can engage the entire line with minimum lateral movement of the weapon. Second, two or more guns should be used to give interlocking arcs of fire, and to engage one target to achieve the best results.

A demonstration of the power of the machine gun in the defence is provided by the experience of a British SAS team at the Omani town of Mirbat in July 1972. The SAS was assisting the Sultan of Oman against communist guerrillas who were trying to overthrow him. The rebels, called *Adoo*, had decided to attack the coastal town of Mirbat to convince the Omani people that their cause would win. Defending Mirbat were a nine-man SAS team, some gendarmes and a handful of SAS-trained militia called *Firqat*.

The town itself was surrounded by a barbed wire fence, while the main defensive

Above: The GPMG mounted on a tripod for sustained fire. Note the dial sight, which allows the gunner to fire blind if necessary.

Above: British Paras manning a 0.5in Browning, the finest heavy machine gun in the world. It has a range of over 6km (3.7 miles) and its bullet is a formidable man-stopper.

positions were the Dhofar Gendarmerie Fort, the Wali's Fort and the British Army Training Team (BATT) house, which was the home of the SAS soldiers. Beside the BATT house was an 81mm mortar pit, while on the roof was a sandbagged strongpoint holding a GPMG and 0.5in Browning heavy machine gun. The town and forts were attacked by over 250 *Adoo* armed with automatic weapons and rocket launchers. One of the SAS troopers, Soldier 'I', manned the Browning and later wrote of the effect the machine gun fire had on the enemy as the battle began: 'We opened fire simultaneously, unleashing a hail of GPMG and .50-calibre bullets at the assaulting *Adoo* troops. The running figures became a focal point where the red tracer and exploding incendiary rounds converged in a frenzied dance. It rained fire and lead. Where moments before there had been an orderly advance, parts of the line now fal-

tered and collapsed. Figures staggered under the impact of the heavy .50-calibre rounds, falling, twisting, screaming. We traversed the machine guns right, a burst of fire scything a lethal harvest among the exposed enemy. But still the *Adoo* kept coming.'

The SAS soldiers and their allies managed to hold on with the help of a couple of Omani ground-attack aircraft and SAS reinforcements, the latter composed of 23 troopers, who had five GPMGs between them. The Battle of Mirbat stands as a testimony to the weapons skills of elite soldiers. At the end of the action, the SAS machine guns on the BATT house roof had become so hot and fouled that the Browning could only be used in single-shot mode.

The 0.5in Browning heavy machine gun used by the SAS at Mirbat is one of the best rapid-fire weapons in the world. Though now over 70 years old, it is robust, reliable, accurate and capable of piercing light armour. When mounted on a tripod the combination weighs in at 59kg (128lb), but in such a mode it has an effective range of over 6km (3.7 miles)! Compared to other machine guns its rate of fire is not that high – 500 rounds per minute – but the rounds it fires have a high velocity and make it extremely unlikely that anyone hit by one will survive.

Other machine guns popular among elite forces include the aforementioned M60. This is a gas-operated weapon, which means that as the round travels down the barrel it pushes gas into the gas cylinder through a hole in the bore. The pressure generated in the cylinder then forces a piston down the chamber, moving the bolt back and bringing the next round into place. After the bullet is fired the process continues as long as the trigger is depressed. The lack of a gas regulator, though, can lead to problems. In Vietnam this caused dust and dirt to accumulate, which slowed down the piston and either jammed the weapon or caused it to 'run away'. The latter meant it would continue to fire even if the finger was not on the trigger. To cure this the assistant gunner had to physically prevent ammunition feeding.

But the M60 does have redeeming features. Chief among these is the quick-change barrel. In addition, the barrel itself is lined with stellite, a non-ferrous material which increases its lifespan. The current version is the M60E1, which has the attachment of the bipod to the rear of the gas cylinder, a modified rear sight and a new feed tray. There is also a lighter M60E3, which has a front pistol grip and revised fore-end.

The Belgian FN MAG, GPMG in British service, is a machine gun that has seen wide service around the world. Still used by the British and Australian SAS, its 7.62mm round

Below: A US Ranger armed with an M249 Squad Automatic Weapon – the Belgian Minimi. It is a light machine gun popular among British and American elite forces.

gives it a greater range and lethality than its 5.56mm rivals. During the 1991 Gulf War, SAS Land Rover patrols which operated behind Iraqi lines had GPMGs fixed to their vehicles for defence.

Though it is an automatic weapon, the GPMG, like most machine guns, is most effective when fired in bursts. For one thing, short bursts allows the firer to correct his aim to take into consideration range and windage. To assist further, it is standard to have tracer as one round in four. Short bursts make the weapon easier to control, especially if firing from a bipod, and rapid fire will cause its barrel to overheat, affecting accuracy. In the sustained fire role – mounted on a tripod – the GPMG has to be properly balanced to ensure the ideal gas regulator setting, which will guarantee reliability and minimum

vibration. The gas pressure should push the working parts far enough back to enable automatic fire, but not too far back to cause extra vibration and wear. A properly balanced GPMG can put around 20 rounds within a circle 500mm (20in) wide at a range of 100m (320ft).

In general, Russian (and Soviet) forces have proven to be less enamoured of the GPMG concept, and have kept separate light machine gun designs in service. When Russian forces incorporated the original AK-47 with its intermediate-power 7.62mm ammunition, they developed a squad-level light machine gun to supplement the rifle's firepower. The RPK is effectively a 'heavy duty' AK, using the same basic mechanism and ammunition. It has a longer, heavier barrel, a bipod and a deeper 'club-shaped'

Below: A typical special forces mortar pit. Both British and American elite teams have used mortars to devastating effect, particularly in the defence of fortified camps.

butt. Weighing only 5.6kg (12.3lb), it is easily carried by one man, and uses the same ammunition as the squad's rifles, thus easing any supply problems. But this is also its weakness, as the intermediate cartridge is optimised for short and medium ranges, and lacks the power for long-range work. The RPK is also hampered by its feed system, as it normally uses 30- or 40-round box magazines, which militate against sustained firepower. The 40-shot item is also rather long and cumbersome, making the weapon difficult to fire from a prone position. There is also a 75-shot drum, although this is rarely seen in use. And while the barrel is heavier than that of the rifle, it is permanently attached, so overheating can be a problem. Nevertheless, the RPK (and other such box-fed light machine guns) can be used by elite teams in a fast-moving assault, especially in urban terrain, where a belt-fed weapon may be awkward to handle.

Russian Machine Guns

As the AK-47 has been developed into the 5.45mm AK-74, the RPK has likewise been updated as the RPK-74. The 5.45mm weapon is effective at slightly longer ranges than its predecessor, although it suffers the same disadvantages in terms of providing sustained firepower.

The Soviets were aware of these shortcomings from the start, and in the 1960s produced a belt-fed GPMG-type weapon, known as the PKM. This fires the full-power 7.62mm cartridge, also used on the Dragunov sniper rifle, and which was first used in the late nineteenth century. At 9kg (19.8lb) the gas-operated PKM is lighter than the M60 and likewise comes complete with a folding bipod. It can also be mounted on vehicles, or on a tripod for the sustained fire role. It has a quick-change barrel, and a 200-shot belt-box can be attached for mobile operations. The PKM fires rimmed ammunition fed from a non-disintegrating belt, which means that the fresh round has to be fully withdrawn to the rear of the belt before the weapon can feed,

a potential source of problems. But in practice, the PKM has proven to be extremely reliable and effective; it has seen service in Vietnam and anywhere else where armies use Russian small arms. When tested by the US Army the PKM was praised for its toughness, reliability and simplicity, and in fact many preferred it to the M60.

Above: The best 81mm mortar in the world, the British L16 model, as used by British and American special forces.

Above: Ban Me Thout Camp, Vietnam, one of the dozens of camps built by US Green Berets during the Vietnam War. The flimsy barricades were designed to impede enemy troops. Then the defenders' heavy weapons would open up.

Machine guns are an integral part of special forces warfare, but if anything the mortar is even more effective. However, it has to be properly positioned and used. There are various calibres of mortars currently in service around the world, but 81mm is one of the most popular with elite units, being used by the French, Americans and British. An 81mm mortar is a smoothbore, muzzle-loading, high-angle-fire weapon which consists of a barrel, base plate and bipod. The great attribute of the mortar is that it combines mobility and firepower in greater degree than other supporting weapon. Its bombs, for example, have an explosive effect comparable to 75mm artillery shells.

Though the mortar can be manhandled – the barrel, bipod and base plate can be separated and carried – it is in defensive positions that the mortar has proved its worth to elite units. Most mortars fire two main types of bomb: smoke and high explosive. The latter

bomb has an effective burst radius of around 35m (110ft).

A well trained mortar crew can fire between 30 and 35 rounds per minute for short periods. A sustained rate of fire is around 18 rounds per minute, though obviously the supply of ammunition will govern the rate of fire. The high trajectory fire of the mortar makes it ideal for use against enemy troops behind cover, be it slopes, rivers, wooded areas and ravines. The large burst radius of the mortar shell also means it can be used to search an enemy occupied area in which the targets are so well concealed by cover that they cannot be located, such as in jungle areas. And because of its high trajectory, mortar fire is not restricted by the safety precautions imposed upon flat-trajectory weapons, when the troops using them are firing over the heads of friendly forces. Mortar crews can continue to support an advance until friendly troops are only 200m

(650ft) from the enemy (and even closer with near-vertical barrels).

The most important considerations when positioning mortars are the location of the enemy to be fired upon and the position of friendly forces, the demands of cover and observation, and routes of ammunition supply. Obviously, mortars must be within range of their targets, and they should be placed within at least 800m (2600ft) of any friendly troops to lend support. Targets at which mortars normally fire are usually within a strip of ground 200-600m (650-1950ft) in front of the friendly frontline. The mortars are invariably situated in protected positions, not in the open, and are also placed far enough away from other heavy weapons and command posts to ensure that a direct hit does not destroy more than one mortar and its crew.

In an attack, mortars fire on enemy targets, which have been identified, but which are protected from the fire of flat-trajectory weapons (area targets that require zone fires are targets for artillery rather than for mortars). Though there may be many potential mortar targets, the special forces unit commander must be mindful of the supply of ammunition and allocate accordingly. Among the targets particularly suited to mortars are enemy troops resting, especially on railway embankments and reverse slopes, and the crews of entrenched heavy weapons. Smoke rounds are used to lay down a screen or blind enemy observers. Illumination rounds are used at night to locate enemy movement or positions for engagement by other direct fire weapons.

As stated above, mortars come into their own with elite units when they are used in defence. In such a scenario the mortars are used to cover dead spaces, which cannot be engaged by machine-gun fire. Each mortar crew is usually given a primary and sec-

Below: A typical special forces fortified camp, based on those built by US Green Berets in Vietnam. The outer defences include belts of barbed wire (A) and punji stakes (B). All machine-gun posts (C) had interlocking arcs of fire, while the mortars (D) were sited to break up enemy attacks before they reached the wire.

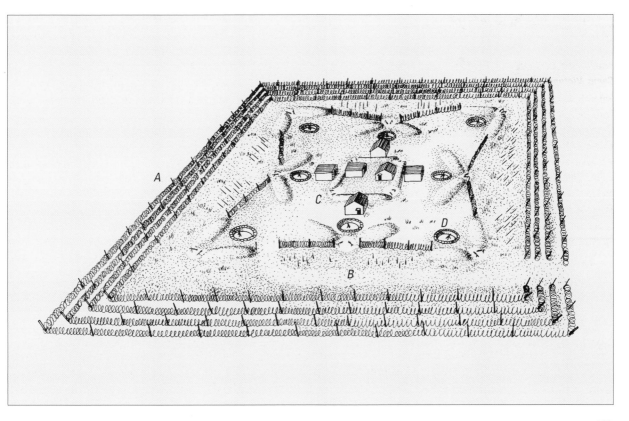

ondary target, or even a number of secondary targets. The primary target is usually an area 100 metres square (320 feet square), within which is an important gap that is not covered by machine guns or other flat-trajectory weapons, such as jungle, a ravine or a stream, along which an enemy may make an approach.

One of the best 81mm mortars currently in service with special forces is the British model. It is very accurate due to the fine limits to which the rounds are machined, and there is an 'obdurating ring' on the round which cuts down on yaw as the shell travels up the barrel. This means that the beaten zone (the area where shells fall after being fired at the same elevation and bearing) is small. Among the disadvantages of the 81mm mortar (and indeed all mortars) is that the relatively low muzzle velocity and the high elevation of the barrel result in the round

being in the air for a considerable amount of time, which means that gusts of wind can affect its accuracy. In addition, the mortar's range can be reduced by damp or water in the barrel, and the lack of any recoil system means that it must be fired from firm ground. Mortars are also very vulnerable to being spotted, either by sound or mortar-locating radars; another reason for siting them in dead ground.

Once mortars have been positioned they have to be laid. They must have a common starting or reference point to which both the commander and individual mortar controllers can refer. In this way fire can be adjusted and coordinated from the different mortar positions. To do this the mortarmen align the crosshairs on their sights with an aiming stick planted in the ground in front of them. Target range and direction, windage and elevation are fed into the mortars by

Below: A Green Beret mortar position in Vietnam. When their bases were attacked, the Green Beret mortarmen used to 'walk' mortar fire around the camp perimeter and onto the enemy soldiers.

dialling the correct number of increments of elevation and azimuth angle into the sight, after a few bedding-in rounds have been fired to ensure a firm base.

Some of the finest examples of how mortars have helped elite troops achieve victory come from the Vietnam conflict, specifically in the fighting camps of the Green Berets' Civilian Irregular Defense Group (CIDG) Program in the Central Highlands of Vietnam. As well as training and raising local Montagnard militia units, the Green Berets established a number of fighting camps. These reached their apogee in the 5th Special Forces Group 1967 CIDG camp construction programme.

Green Beret Fighting Camps

The Green Beret fighting camp was characterised by simplicity. It was in effect a miniature fortress, with positions providing mutual support and the camp having defence in depth. Each camp was surrounded by at least four belts of barbed wire or razor wire, with outlying fields of fire cleared with defoliants or fire. A line of Claymore mines covered the perimeter, and there were sandbagged mortar and machine-gun positions and revetments to provide cover. The focal point of the camp was a number of strongpoints, each covering the other, connected by trenches. The centre of the camp housed the tactical operations centre, communications bunker, medical bunker and sometimes a helipad. The strongpoints themselves contained mortars and machine guns.

Defended camps proved extremely difficult to take by force, as the Viet Cong (VC) and NVA found out to their cost, and even if the defences were not as strong as they could be due to various reasons. The Special Forces camp at Plei Mrong, situated on the highland plateau of Kontum, was attacked by the VC on the morning of 3 January 1963. Though this camp was not as strong as those constructed later, its defences were in a reasonable state, with an outer perimeter constructed of two double barbed wire

fences, steel spikes and the ground between the two wires filled with anti-personnel mines and wooden punji stakes.

On the morning of the 3rd a VC company infiltrated through a gap in the perimeter cut by pro-VC elements in the local militia and began firing and throwing grenades into the trenches. Alerted to the danger, the on-site Green Berets raced to their positions. Four of them jumped into the 81mm mortar pit and began returning fire. For two and a half hours the battle raged in and around the camp, with two VC attacks being defeated in front of the mortar pit. The VC eventually pulled back their troops, their final assault being made at 0600 hours. The battle of Plei Mrong had cost the lives of 29 camp defenders and a further 38 wounded, and all four Green Berets had been wounded in the mortar pit.

One of the most impressive examples of combined mortar and machine-gun fire in the hands of elite troops occurred at the camp of Nam Dong in July 1964. The Green Beret A-Team A-726 was deployed to the camp in Thua Thien Province and was situated along a major VC infiltration route. The camp itself consisted of an inner and outer perimeter, though because it was being closed down, high, thick elephant grass had been allowed to grow right up to the barbed wire perimeter.

The Situation at Nam Dong

The Green Beret commander, Captain Roger Donlon, had inherited a delicate situation. The 50 Nung mercenaries were loyal to the 12 members of the A-Team, but were at odds with the 381 members of the South Vietnamese Montagnard CIDG personnel. This animosity had even erupted into a firefight over a local prostitute. But worse was to follow. In the early hours of 6 July 1964, a reinforced VC battalion crossed the river and the airstrip and approached the camp. The enemy's first act was to silence the 20-man outpost guarding the airstrip. Then the VC approached the camp perimeter, using the elephant grass for cover.

Right: Captain Roger Donlon photographed after his epic defence of Nam Dong, Vietnam, in July 1964. The Green Berets' mortar and machine-gun fire beat off a full battalion of Viet Cong soldiers.

At 0230 hours the first salvo of VC mortar fire destroyed the Nung barracks, the medical shelter and the communications bunker. Then enemy mortar rounds blew apart the Green Beret communications hut, though not before a hurried message had been sent.

As the VC pressed home their attack, Donlon raced over to the 81mm mortar pit, where the weapon was being manned by Staff Sergeant Merwin Woods. The latter began 'walking' a line of 81mm mortar fire around the perimeter. Meanwhile, Sergeant John Houston, armed with an M60 machine gun, was engaged in a close-quarter firefight with VC elements occupying nearby ammunition bunkers. His tactic was ingenious: he would scurry around his large mound of dirt that was his position and fire at the attackers from different angles, thereby making them

believe he was more than just a single man. However, he was alone and soon surrounded, eventually being killed by automatic fire. The VC pressed home their attack, killing a further two A-Team members. However, the small arms and mortar fire of the Americans gave them enough time for a relief force to arrive, and the camp was saved.

Another impressive display of mortar and machine gun fire occurred at Camp Loc Ninh between 29 October and 4 November 1967. One mass assault which took place on 2 November was destroyed by a combination of Claymores, small arms fire, mortars and aircraft strafing runs. The defensive fire was so intense that the VC left behind 1000 of their comrades dead around the camp. By comparison, four Green Berets were lightly wounded, six CIDG killed and a further 39 wounded.

THE FIGHTING SKILLS IN ACTION

CHAPTER 10

AMBUSHES

The ambush is without doubt one of the most effective weapons in the special forces armoury. However, ambushes require detailed prior planning, expert siting and perfect timing to achieve maximum effectiveness. But when all the ingredients come together the results are spectacular.

Among the plethora of elite unit tactics, the ambush is the most effective. This chapter will examine how special forces formations spring ambushes to annihilate enemy formations. But first of all, the ambush itself must be described and explained.

Put simply, an ambush is a surprise attack on an enemy formation with the intention of destroying it. It combines maximum firepower with minimum time, and does not require the attacking force to take or hold territory. Afterwards the ambushers make a rapid withdrawal. During the actual ambush each attacking soldier is usually given his own arc of fire, which overlaps with other arcs of fire to ensure there are no gaps. The key to an ambush is shock action: a quick kill followed by a speedy withdrawal. The action should be over within two minutes maximum, though elite units often finish the job in less than 30 seconds.

The withdrawal is integral to the success of the ambush, as enemy reinforcements may be closing fast. To this end, guides are often posted at points behind the ambush site to show the ambushers towards safety (this is especially true at night). The most effective type of operation is the deliberate ambush, where prior intelligence has allowed the ambushers to plan their actions. With knowledge concerning the size, composition and organisation of an enemy force, together with the time it will arrive at the ambush site, an ambush party can plan an effective attack. An ambush without prior intelligence, such as where an enemy force has just been spotted, is usually termed an ambush of opportunity.

Left: Troops of the US 82nd Airborne Division set Claymores during an ambush exercise. The Claymore is integral to many elite unit ambushes.

The target will obviously determine the nature of the force employed and the size of the ambush force. An ambush against enemy troops on foot is considered one of the most difficult because trained enemy troops are always aware of the dangers of being ambushed while on the move, and are therefore very alert. In addition, they usually throw out security elements to their front, flanks and rear. Against poorly armed and trained opponents an elite ambush has a better chance, but even poor-quality large formations will be treated with respect because it is extremely difficult to wipe out the entire unit in one attempt, and the enemy will often mount a hasty counterattack. Ambushes against vehicles, be they armoured or unarmoured, are easier, as the speed at which the vehicles travel makes little difference once they have been stopped. Vehicle convoys often have poorly guarded flanks, and once the lead and rear vehicles have been disabled any troops acting as convoy security become targets for automatic weapons. Ambushing riverine craft is very similar to attacking vehicle con-

voys, especially when boats are moving along narrow waterways.

The actual ambushing force is made up of three parts: the command element, the assault element and the security element. The command element usually comprises the commander, radio operators and medics.

The assault element has the task of destroying the enemy in the actual ambush, and is composed of assault teams, support teams and special task teams.

The assault teams spring the ambush, with the support teams providing back-up with machine guns and mortars, and stopping enemy personnel escaping the killing zone. The job of the special task teams is to kill sentries, lay mines and carry out searches. The latter are sometimes conducted after an ambush and involve searching the dead for documents and other intelligence.

The security element does just that: provide security. It covers all areas of approach that the enemy might use to reinforce the ambushed party, and it also covers the withdrawal of the ambushers and acts as a rearguard. It may also cover possible withdrawal

Right: US 101st Airborne Division personnel practising ambush drills. Elite unit ambushes are usually over in 30 seconds or less.

routes for enemy forces who have managed to escape the killing zone. In many ways the security element is one of the most important parts of the operation, for it protects the vulnerable flanks of the ambushing force. Security around the ambush site itself must be strictly maintained at all times until the moment when the ambush is sprung. But what about the disposition of the ambush party itself?

The most common types of ambush formations are the linear, L-shaped, V-shaped, demolition and pinwheel varieties. When laying an ambush it is assumed that the commander knows the direction from which the enemy is coming, but he will nevertheless ensure that his ambush site has all-round security to provide early warning of a threat from an unexpected direction.

The Linear Ambush

The linear ambush is one of the simplest ambushes, though no less effective than the others. It uses heavy flank firepower to destroy the enemy in the killing zone, while flank and rear security provides cover against a surprise attack. With all the firepower going forward, the linear ambush is easy to control; it is often sprung where it is difficult for the ambushed to move off the road or trail, such as where there is a steep hill on the opposite side of the road. In addition, mines, Claymores and booby traps can be used to keep the ambushed in the killing zone. However, the linear ambush does have disadvantages, chief among them being that it is easy to flank the ambushers and a linear method is hard to employ against large formations. When planning the linear ambush, the commander must ensure that his assault elements are parallel to the enemy force. If they are not, and the ambush line engages just the head of the enemy unit –- known as 'crossing the T' – then the rear elements of the opponent's unit will be able to outflank the ambushers.

The L-shaped ambush employs fire from two directions, and is highly effective along

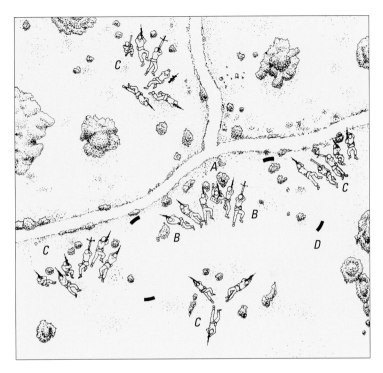

curves and bends in roads and tracks or, even better, along rivers and canals. When setting up the ambush positions, the long side of the 'L' is usually parallel to the expected route of the target. Automatic weapons are traditionally placed in the centre of each side of the 'L' to give increased overlap of fire, i.e. a crossfire. In an L-shaped ambush, the commander can employ staggered fire. In this situation one leg of the assault force opens fire first, giving the impression that a linear ambush has been sprung; then the second leg opens fire. Against a vehicle convoy, for example, the first leg opens fire with mortars and anti-tank rockets, while the second leg uses automatic fire against any enemy personnel who disembark from their vehicles.

The V-shaped ambush, if used correctly, can be extremely damaging to an enemy unit. Its advantage lies in the fact that it denies the ambushed a safe area in any direction. For example, if they fire towards the front they can be killed from the rear; if they wheel around to deal with the danger behind them they can be killed by frontal

Above: A typical special forces ambush (not to scale) showing the constituent parts of the ambush party: the command element (A), the assault element (B) and security elements (C). Claymore mines (D) are used in the ambush and for security.

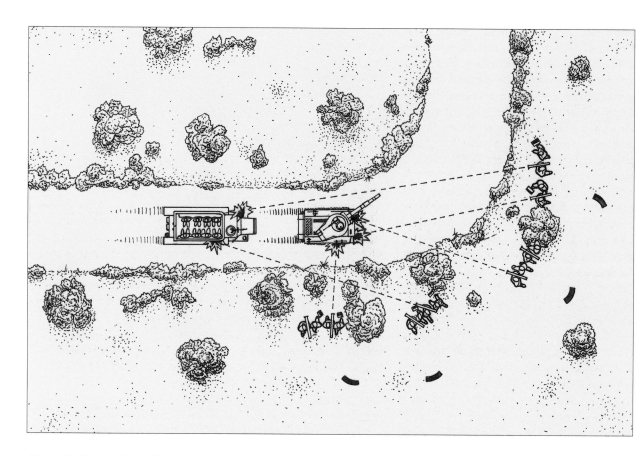

Above: The L-shaped ambush (not to scale), which employs fire from two directions and is usually set along curves and bends in roads.

fire. The main problem with this type of ambush is that friendly fire may kill or wound members of the ambush party, because each side of the 'V' is shooting inwards. A way round this problem is for the ambushers to be shooting downwards so any misaimed rounds go into the ground. Sometimes an ambush commander will employ only demolitions, such as Claymores and grenades, to spring his ambush. This, the demolition ambush, avoids any use of small-arms fire and thus minimises the chance of friendly casualties – it is also expedient against a numerically superior enemy who has greater firepower. This type of ambush is sprung by the commander in the rear, out of small-arms range, receiving intelligence from spotters who advise him when the enemy is in the killing zone.

The so-called pinwheel ambush is unusual in that it is used when the ambushers do not know the exact direction from which the enemy is coming. The pinwheel formation allows great flexibility and gives good rear and flank security. However, no matter what type of ambush is used, the ambushers must know as much as possible about the enemy's strength, route, tactics and so on to ensure a successful ambush. And one of the most important aspects of ambushing is selecting the ambush site. Elite troops will avoid ideal ambush sites because they will also be obvious to the enemy. When choosing an ambush site, special forces will be determined by four governing factors: the site must allow the enemy to be channelled into a killing zone, it must have good fields of fire, it must accommodate concealed positions, and it must have covered routes of rapid withdrawal.

The planning for an ambush is split into three elements: planning considerations, intelligence and the selection of sites. Planning involves determining what type of ambush is required for the task. For example, an ambush against a vehicle convoy with the aim of destroying all the vehicles and killing all enemy personnel will require a command element, assault element, security element and specialised groups, such as squads to supply heavy automatic fire. This leads on to considerations of numbers and terrain (ideally the ambushers want unobserved routes of approach and withdrawal). Timing is one of the most important aspects of the ambush. One sprung in conditions of low light, for example, will achieve more surprise and confusion than one sprung in daylight. That said, daylight ambushes are much easier to control and allow offensive action to continue for longer.

Intelligence is perhaps the most important element in the planning of ambushes. The ambushers need to reconnoitre the ground, survey the general area and the ambush site itself, being careful not to give the enemy any clues that an ambush is going to take place. In addition to this, the special forces commander will collect intelligence on the composition, strength and time of arrival of the convoy or group to be ambushed. Once this has been determined, the ambush commander will go about selecting the ambush site itself. When timely and accurate intelligence is collected and disseminated properly, the results can be spectacular. In June 1988, for example, British intelligence services in Northern Ireland collected information that a former Ulster Defence Regiment (UDR) officer was going to be assassinated by an Irish Republican Army (IRA) hit squad. The elite British SAS, working with the Royal Ulster Constabulary (RUC) and the various intelligence agencies, decided to set an ambush. The intended victim of the IRA attack was informed of the operation, and he

Below: The pinwheel ambush, used when the direction of approach of the enemy is not known. When the enemy (A) is ambushed, the half of the ambush party covering the other direction (B) deploys to support the actual ambush party (C).

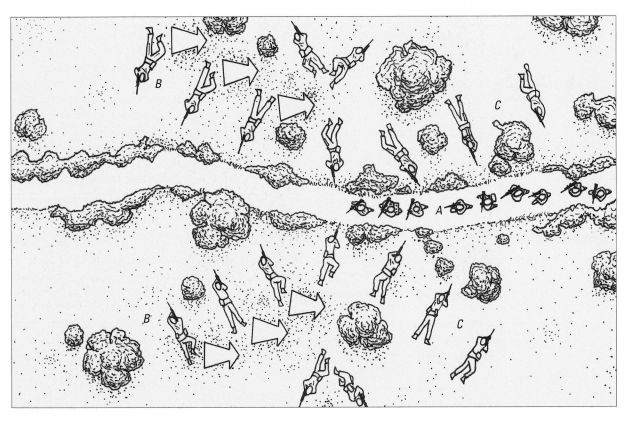

Above: An ideal ambush target. Bunched and exposed, these men would be cut down in seconds.

Drumnakilly. The soldiers were armed with Heckler & Koch MP5 submachine guns, which have a high rate of fire, and they took up positions either side of the road. The truck with its SAS driver arrived soon afterwards, and he unloaded the spare tyre and tools to give the impression that he was changing a flat tyre. Soon afterwards a white car sped into view – the car containing three IRA terrorists. The SAS truck driver dived for cover and the car screeched to a halt. The terrorists jumped out and began spraying automatic gunfire in the direction of the driver behind a wall. At that moment the concealed SAS soldiers opened fire with their submachine guns. In a few seconds all three terrorists had been killed, the SAS soldiers obeying the ambushers' law: shoot fast, shoot last, shoot to kill.

The Ambush Site

The site should have most of the following attributes to make it an ideal location for an ambush: it should channel the target, it should have good fields of fire, it should have good cover for the ambush party, there should be natural obstacles to hinder the ambushed from escaping, and it should have concealed approach and withdrawal routes. The most ideal site is one that at first appears to be an unlikely ambush site, but in reality offers the attackers a killing zone where the defenders can be quickly eliminated. Natural obstacles such as cliffs, streams and embankments will force a column of men or vehicles to slow down, as will man-made restrictions: mines, cratered roads and barbed wire.

For the assault element, firing positions should have a thin screen of foliage in front for concealment purposes, and the entire killing zone should be covered by fire to prevent any dead space. American military manuals had the following to say about selection of ambush sites during the Vietnam War: 'Ambushes are most effective when the site selected confines the VC [Viet Cong] to an area where he can be destroyed. Natural obstacles are numerous in Vietnam for

volunteered to continue to drive his Leyland truck to work along his regular route. In this way a pattern was set, around which, it was hoped, the terrorists would base their plans. This was the bait.

On 29 August 1988, the terrorists were observed travelling to their concealed arms cache, which meant the attack was going to be carried out the next day. Therefore, a disguised SAS soldier took the place of the driver and drove the truck to the ambush site. At the same time, a three-man SAS team left the barracks in Omagh and headed for a disused farmhouse near the village of ambush positions, such as cliffs, embankments, and narrow trails and roads with canals on either side. An indirect approach should be used to enter the ambush site, otherwise the VC will detect the friendly movement and deploy against GVN [Government of Vietnam] forces. At times, use of a circuitous route may require three or four days to reach the ambush site. A patrol may be forced to occupy an ambush site well ahead of the arrival of the target. Patience is essential if secrecy is to be maintained. Therefore, units must be prepared to remain in ambush areas for a minimum of a week and often as long as a month.'

There is a great deal of work to be done in actually springing the ambush. For example, the commander must always thoroughly reconnoitre the ambush site himself before the action to ensure that everything is in order. Once he has decided the ambush is going ahead, he then moves up his forces. The first to assume their positions are the flank groups – it is essential that the flanks are covered before the main assault element moves into place, to ensure that the ambushers have a good view of anything approaching. Then the assault element moves into place.

It is extremely important that automatic weapons, especially machine guns, are placed to ensure their left and right arcs of fire are fixed to safeguard against hitting any friendly personnel, particularly flank elements. Once troops are in place it is essential to maintain noise discipline, which involves keeping movement to a minimum. And discipline in general must be high, which means no smoking, sleeping or talking.

Machine guns are often placed in the centre of the assault element so that they can cover the entire killing zone with gunfire. In this case, their ammunition supply is placed in a box and not on the ground; this keeps noise down and keeps the rounds dry and clean (the machine gunners will often use tracer when the ambush is sprung to delineate the extent of the killing zone).

The flank elements play an integral part in springing the ambush, for it is they who communicate the presence of the enemy, either by word or by means of a tug line that

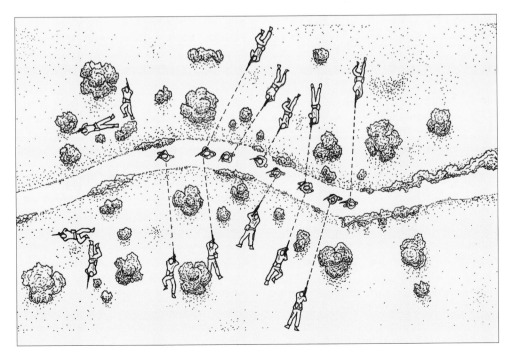

Left: The V-shaped ambush (not to scale), which denies the ambushed party a safe area in any direction by having wide arcs of fire.

Above: The Claymore mine, which upon detonation can scatter 350 steel balls in a 60-degree arc up to a range of 50m (160ft).

Anything else, such as a whistle, will give the enemy time to react. At this signal the assault element will remove their safety catches (all safety catches are kept on until the last minute to prevent accidental discharges) and open fire. Each member of the assault element will fire into predesignated areas to ensure the enemy is enveloped in fire. In a vehicle ambush the first and last vehicles are disabled first so the rest are trapped between them. The actual firing is conducted at close ranges to ensure that maximum damage is inflicted. As well as automatic fire, shotguns and grenades may be used – anything that increases overall saturation of the target. If the ambush takes place at night, flares and other illumination will be used to light up the target.

Ambush Firepower

The rate of fire is high and directed at all enemy personnel – no one gets out alive. In the case of vehicles, anti-tank rounds and rockets will be used both to disable the vehicles and kill those inside them (the last two or three rounds in small arms magazines should be tracer to notify the firer that he is about to run out of rounds and can prepare to reload). But when does an ambush end?

The commander will bring the ambush to an end for three reasons: all the enemy have been killed, the enemy has been mauled and is retreating, or the ambush has been unsuccessful. If all the enemy have been killed, the commander may authorise a walk-through of the killing zone, which is conducted speedily. The noise generated by the ambush may have alerted other enemy forces, or reinforcements may already be on their way. Either way, the commander will wish to evacuate the ambush site quickly. This is done in stages, with the assault element pulling out first and the security element covering. When pulling out, the idea is to create maximum deception as the various elements withdraw to their rallying points. If the enemy is pursuing, the security element will use fire and movement to slow them

is strung between the members of the ambush team. But this is not the signal for firing to begin – only the commander can decide that; rather, it is to help the commander decide what course of action to take. In short-range ambushes this decision will often be made on sight, but where the range is longer it will be on a predetermined signal or when the target reaches a predetermined point. The most important consideration will be if the target is in the killing zone (a premature ambush will fail to annihilate the enemy and may even endanger the ambush party). The ambush will not take place if less than 90 per cent of the target is in the killing zone, because 10 per cent of an enemy force is reckoned to give him too much freedom to outflank the ambush party and mount a successful counter-ambush.

When it comes to actually springing the ambush, nothing other than a weapon or explosive device will be used, i.e. something that will inflict casualties on the enemy.

down. In the case of a pursuit the various elements of the ambush party may split into small groups to evade the pursuers.

Sometimes ambushes will be sprung using demolitions only. A demolition ambush is one in which there is no assault element other than personnel triggering the explosives themselves. These types of ambushes are very useful when the aim is the destruction of part of a convoy or column, or even just one vehicle. But in planning demolition ambushes the commander has to take in some special considerations. These are that the best location is a road or track bordered by woods, brush, swamp or water, and preferably on a hill or curve. When negotiating such obstacles, columns are slowed down, making them more vulnerable to attack and giving more time for the triggering of explosives. Prior knowledge of the enemy's movements and time of arrival are crucial to demolition ambushes, and the commander must ensure the proper placement of mines, fragmentation charges and demolitions.

One of the greatest aids to a demolition ambush, and ambushes in general, is the Claymore mine. The Claymore is a directional fragmentation mine designed primarily for anti-personnel use, though it can also be employed against soft-skinned vehicles, where its fragments will pierce the outer shell and injure the occupants. They will also puncture tyres, petrol tanks and radiators. When the mine is detonated, up to 350 steel fragments are scattered in a fan-shaped pattern over a 60-degree spherical horizontal arc, inflicting casualties over an area of 50m (160ft) at a height of 2m (6ft).

The effectiveness of the Claymore in an ambush is illustrated by the comments of a Green Beret veteran who fought in Vietnam: 'When the enemy did at last arrive, the prime weapon the assault element used to destroy him was not the M16 rifle, it was the 2.5lb [1.1kg] Claymore anti-personnel mine. The Claymore did the killing. The spread on that weapon was about 60 degrees and the optimum effective range was about 50yds, although in close terrain with trees and other obstacles it would be less, and you would need more mines to do the job. Let's say you needed three Claymores for a 20- to 30-man

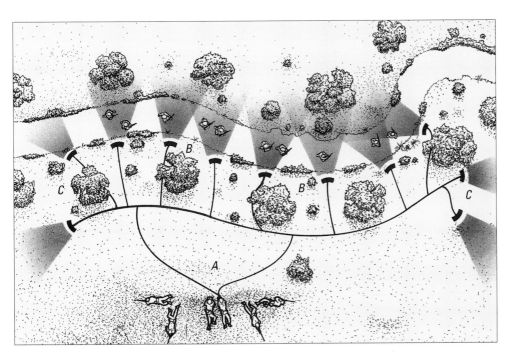

Left: The Claymore ambush. Triggered by a command group in the rear (A), some Claymores saturate the killing zone with lethal fragments (B), while others provide flank security (C).

Indeed, it provides firepower out of all proportion to the size of the ambush party. However, Claymores take time to set, and the commander must be careful as to their placement. The detonator cord and wires, for example, must be camouflaged. In addition, firing wires must not be wrapped around the legs of mines as someone will undoubtedly walk into them and pull them over. It is crucial to use a dual initiation circuit: a blasting cap in both detonator wells and two separate circuits. Similarly, it is important not to place Claymores in front of trees as they can come crashing down when the mines are detonated. The commander must also be careful not to let his radio operators transmit messages near the mines as their signals may set them off. Finally, all members of the ambush party must be behind cover and at least 16m (50ft) behind or to the side of all mines. Proper placement requires time, but the terrain itself can aid the siting of Claymores.

Claymore Ambushes

Claymores can be used in groups where simultaneous detonation is initiated from one point. The first mine is detonated by the firing device and detonator assembly, while succeeding mines are detonated by linking them with detonating cord (the detonating cord must be camouflaged and checked to ensure there is no damage from moisture or fraying). The Claymores can be placed either in a straight line, running parallel to the killing zone, or at an angle of 45 degrees to the killing zone from both the left and right. But what are the actual distances involved in ambushes?

Clearly there are no hard rules regarding the distance between the ambushers and their prey. Factors such as the availability of cover and the weapons skills of the ambush party come into play. During the Vietnam War, for example, VC ambush groups usually opened fire against vehicle columns at a range of between 10-60m (33-100ft).

Ambushes against vehicle convoys and personnel are the most common types of

Above: US inshore patrol craft in Vietnam. Such vessels can be ideal targets for concealed ambush parties on riverbanks.

enemy unit coming down the trail. The assault team would then consist of three Claymore firers who would kick off the mines on signal from the patrol leader, then pick up their M16s fast in case anyone was still fighting in the killing zone. The other two members of the assault element on the flanks of the Claymore firers would start firing their M16s as soon as they got the signal. Few survived such an ambush.'

The Claymore can cover the killing zone with instantaneous firepower, and it can also be used to supplement small-arms fire.

ambush, but attacks on railroads and river traffic are also part of elite unit tactics. These can often reap rich rewards because lines of communications, be they railroads or rivers, are often long and therefore difficult to protect along their whole length. The enemy will simply not have the manpower to cover every metre of track or waterway.

Ambushes against railways centre on the rails themselves. Moving trains can be fired upon, but the aim of the ambush party should be the derailment of the train itself, preferably on a downward grade, a sharp curve or on a high bridge. This will result in the cars overturning and the occupants becoming casualties. When attacking passenger trains, the weapons of the ambush party should be directed at the exits of the overturned coaches (any coaches that remain standing will have to be cleared with automatic fire and grenades if they are carrying military personnel).

After the ambush has taken place, the ambush party should remove the rails from the track at some distance from the ambush site in each direction to slow down the arrival of reinforcements (if the line is double-tracked rails will have to be removed from each set of tracks). The vulnerability of trains is also understood by the enemy, and the ambushing party will do well to remember that there may be armoured railroad cars in the train for its protection. Alternatively, some trains carrying vital supplies or troops may be preceded by advance guard locomotives or inspection cars to check the track.

Ambushes against river vessels also offer rich rewards. Troops positioned along riverbanks and in patrol craft concealed along the banks can be used to carry out ambushes. However, boats are not essential to carry out an ambush: troops on the banks are more than adequate for the job. A stealthy approach is the key when ferrying troops to an ambush site in boats. Paddles or oars should be used instead of motors when inserting an ambush party, and even the tide and currents can be used to aid silent movement along the waterway. However, the motors should always be in a state of readiness to effect a quick getaway or a rapid attack if the target appears.

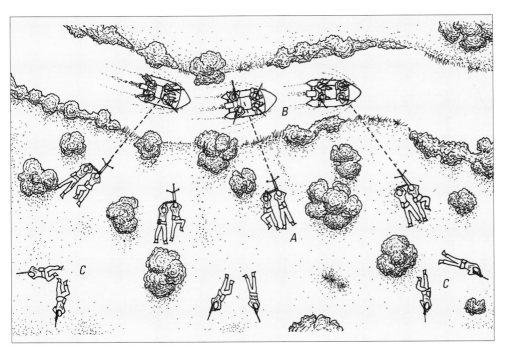

Left: A riverine ambush sprung from the bank. The ambush party (A) hits all the boats at once (B), while other soldiers provide flank and rear security (C).

An American Special Forces manual has the following to say about deployment for a river ambush: 'Several hours of waiting are generally required at any riverine ambush site. During this time, there may be changes of the water level and even the direction of flow of the river or stream. Ambush commanders have to anticipate such changes and plan accordingly. For instance, water-level changes caused by tides may require that weapons be repositioned because of alterations in fields of fire. The direction of approach of the enemy craft may be based on the direction of the current. In an ebbing tide, waterway withdrawal routes may become too shallow to use, or craft may actually be stranded – left high if not necessarily dry. Tidal effects can also make landings across mud flats difficult, affect operations around bridges, and leave some weapons useless for periods of time.'

The actual insertion can be fraught with difficulties. For example, troops inserted at low tide may have to travel through mud that can be waist deep or worse. In Vietnam. for example, there was an average 10m (33ft) tidal change. With regard to the boats themselves, it is important that the commander does not load all his vital personnel and equipment into one boat, leaving him unable to carry out his mission if that boat comes under attack or mechanical failure renders it unusable. Similarly, the commander must ensure that there are separate insertion and extraction points for his force.

If boats are to be used in the actual ambush, the commander must consider a number of factors with regard to the waterway. These are the depth of the water at the ambush site, any obstacles in the water that may affect the approach and withdrawal, tidal changes, weather conditions, concealment along the bank, fields of fire, avenues of approach and, if necessary, illumination requirements. The boats themselves should be secured with light tensile line, which is

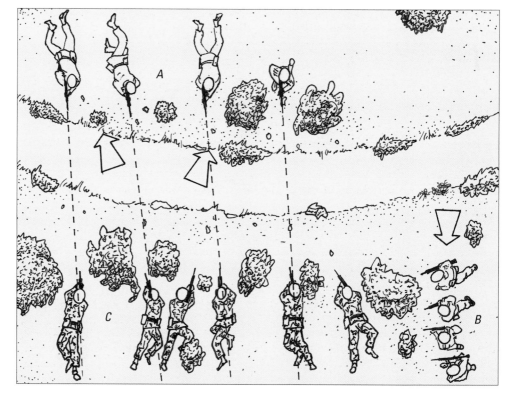

Right: A special forces anti-ambush drill. If only part of the unit is ambushed (A), the others (B) can immediately launch a flank attack against the ambushers (C). Meanwhile, the survivors of those ambushed (A) have taken cover.

Left: A British SAS patrol equipped for an ambush, with weapons that include assault rifles, 66mm anti-tank rockets and M203 grenade launchers.

strong enough to hold the craft against the current. Fields of fire should be worked out early, with each boat being assigned fields of fire, which overlap with those of other boats.

Of course, river ambushes can also be sprung from the bank. Good camouflage and concealment skills can ensure that a land-based team can remain in situ for long periods of time without being detected, and can choose its target with great care.

If ambushes form an essential part of elite unit tactics, so do counter-ambush drills. The key to a successful counter-ambush is hitting back instantaneously. Relief and pursuit are the two most important factors in reducing the effectiveness of an ambush. Immediately hitting back, though undoubtedly risky, does give relief to the ambushed party and cuts down on the time available to the attackers to destroy the ambushed party. There is also the morale factor: a unit which survives an ambush and mounts a successful counterattack is going to bolster morale, and demoralise the foe. At the least, counter-ambush tactics give time for reinforcements to arrive. But what are counter-ambush tactics?

The most important aspect is to keep moving when fired upon, either charging the ambushers in the killing zone itself or passing right through it and then mounting a counterattack from the flanks. If a vehicle convoy is ambushed, the following rules apply: the drivers will keep on driving until they reach positions clear of enemy fire, guards will open fire immediately upon known or suspected ambush positions, as vehicles clear the killing zone they will stop to allow their occupants to disembark and take offensive action, and no vehicles should try to pass through the killing zone which aren't caught in it. Some vehicles will obviously be immediately disabled in the killing zone. In such a case any occupants left alive should dismount and attack. A US Special Forces veteran who fought in Vietnam recalls the tactics used to beat ambushes against vehicles: 'Since we used a lot of armour with our convoys in VC or NVA [North Vietnamese Army] territory, the enemy often bit off more than he could chew. I knew a number of armoured cavalry and tank commanders who just loved to run the roads looking for an ambush. They would immediately counterattack the enemy ambush force, call in artillery and know that helicopter-borne infantry would be on the way.'

Right: Elite unit anti-ambush drill. The ambushed party (A) immediately charges the ambushers (B), laying down intensive small-arms and grenade fire.

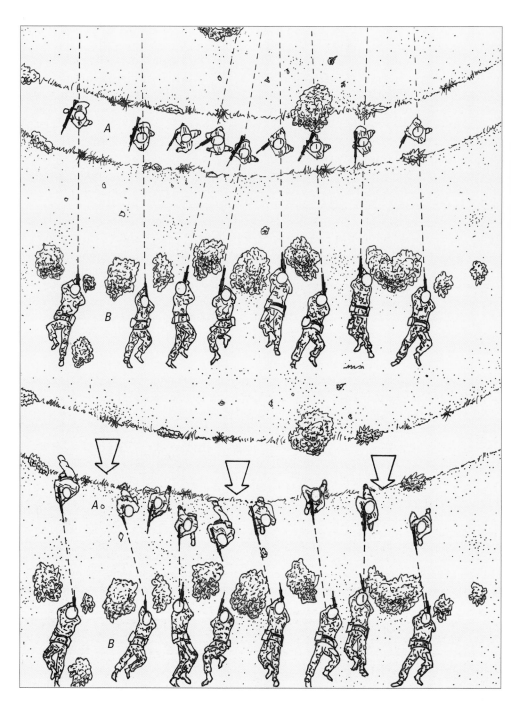

For foot patrols the drill is very similar. A manual on ambushes states the following regarding foot patrols mounting counter-ambushes: 'If ambushed, all troops must be conditioned to react immediately and vio- lently, without orders, to overcome the initial advantage held by the enemy. The immedi- ate-action drills are one example of this reflex-type action. Because an ambush inflicts its casualties almost immediately and no attempt is made to prolong the engagement, an immediate reaction to build and retain fire superiority is the best initial defence against an ambush.' All available firepower should be brought to bear on the ambushers, including automatic fire, explosive and white phosphorous grenades and even anti-tank rockets when available.

The commander of the ambush party should be a prime target in a counter-ambush. He will usually position himself where he can best control the ambush, which is at the point where the head of the column or the patrol must be stopped. Heavy automatic fire directed at this spot may result in the commander becoming a casualty, which may disrupt the ambush's command and control. However, care must be taken not to fall into a trap. A seasoned ambush party can spring an ambush, wait for a counter-ambush to take place and then strike from a different direction with the primary ambush force.

Above all, though, a counter-ambush must be characterised by violent and aggressive action. Particular attention should be paid towards enveloping a flank of the ambush party, preferably by a part of the unit which is not involved in the ambush. Once a threat to its flank materialises, the ambush party will break contact. Once this happens, pursuit operations must be instantaneously launched and pursued with the utmost relentlessness. The proviso in such a case being that a pursuit should only proceed in conditions of good visibility; where it is poor the pursuers should not allow themselves to become separated from the main force and perhaps drawn into another ambush. But keeping an enemy off-balance will allow reinforcements to be called up to press any long-range pursuit.

Left: Elite unit ambushes require much practice to perfect, but at the end of the day the ambush commander's ultimate aim is to 'shoot fast, shoot last, shoot to kill'.

CHAPTER 11

ASSASSINATION

Elite units are not assassins in the true sense of the word. However, some special forces soldiers, particularly Russia's Spetsnaz, do carry out assassinations as part of their operational role, and they carry out their task with their usual ruthlessness, speed and determination.

The Oxford dictionary defines assassination as an act to 'kill for political or religious motives'. Clearly this definition can be applied to all soldiers, not just those belonging to elite units, as all legitimate military formations are killing under orders, be it from a democratically elected government or a military or religious junta, which is acting in accordance with political motives. However extreme the regime, the soldiers who serve it are obeying military law in trying to kill the enemy. That they may stray from the rules of war and commit atrocities does not concern us here; but they cannot be labelled assassins. The reality is that the assassin often operates beyond the law, carrying out work on behalf of governments who can then deny his actions. Then there are the terrorist assassins, such as those who work for organisations like the Irish Republican Army (IRA) in Northern Ireland and Eire. They assassinate in pursuance of a cause. IRA operatives assassinated a member of the British Royal Family, Earl Mountbatten, in 1979 while on holiday in the Irish Republic. This was a political act, as was the assassination of the Chechen leader Dzhokar Dudayev in April 1996, killed by a rocket fired by a Russian aircraft. A more suitable example of an assassin would be Colonel Eugene de Kock of the South African police, who was found guilty at the end of October 1996 for murders committed on behalf of the South African Government in the era before majority rule. Acting at the behest of his political masters, including President P. W. Botha, who wanted the fight to be taken to the African National Congress, de Kock ran a police death squad at the Vlakplaas, a 100-acre former farm outside

Left: US Navy SEALs, who during the Vietnam War in the 1960s undertook assassination missions as part of the so-called Phoenix Program.

Pretoria until its closure in 1993. The Vlakplaas squad, called C-10, was officially the police's elite counter-terrorist unit, but in reality the unit had a free hand to kill, torture and embezzle state funds. At his trial de Kock was found guilty of 89 crimes, including six murders, two counts of conspiracy to murder, one of attempted murder, one of culpable homicide and 66 counts of fraud. Among the methods he used to kill people included entrenching tool blows to the head and suffocating individuals with the inner tubes of tyres. In addition, he organised the bombing of Cosatu House, the Johannesburg headquarters of the largest black trade union, in 1987, and shot dead the alleged 'sex slave' of Winnie Mandela, a security force agent named Johan Magota.

Spetsnaz Assassins

There are very few special forces units which are trained from the outset to carry out assassination missions. Many elite formations may be tasked with 'taking out' key enemy figures during strike missions, but this does not deviate from their primary aim of killing enemy personnel in wartime. A semi-official manual commissioned by the US House of Representatives regarding American Special Forces had this to say about assassination: 'Assassination and abduction are illegal special operations employed offensively for socio-political purposes. Official actions to capture or kill key insurgents and transnational terrorists are legal and defensive. The two couplets in some respect are similar. Both call for expert marksmanship, willingness to take human life without hesitation, and professional tracking abilities. It takes less skill to strike lightly defended tactical targets of local value than well protected leaders, whose removal would profoundly affect rival war efforts.'

Russia's Spetsnaz is one of the few units that actually lists assassination among its duties, both in wartime and in peacetime. During the Cold War, the Spetsnaz was trained to infiltrate into the West to carry out

reconnaissance and sabotage missions. The latter included assassinating military and political leaders. As the Soviet Military Encyclopedia stated with regard to Spetsnaz missions: 'Reconnaissance carried out to subvert the political, economic and military potential and morale of a probable or actual enemy. The primary missions of special reconnaissance are: acquiring intelligence on major economic and military installations and either destroying them or putting them out of action; organising sabotage and acts of subversion; carrying out *punitive operations* against rebels; [author's italics] conducting propaganda; forming and training insurgent detachments...'

Assassination in Kabul

The kind of punitive operation mentioned above included wiping out the entire enemy leadership with extreme ruthlessness. An example of a Spetsnaz assassination team is provided by the Soviet invasion of Afghanistan in December 1979. A company led by a KGB officer, Colonel Byeronov, assaulted the palace of President Hazifullah Amin during the Soviet invasion. The preparation and execution of the operation is classic Spetsnaz: the team began arriving at Kabul airport on 24 December, the men dressed in civilian clothing as they left their Aeroflot transports. They achieved a major coup on Christmas Eve when they locked up senior Afghan officers who had been deceived into attending a reception at the Soviet Embassy. The next day, now dressed in Afghan Army uniforms, they secured the airport and its approaches. All that remained was the presidential Darulaman Palace and President Amin.

The next phase of the Spetsnaz operation represents a clear example of strategic assassination: the denial of opponents' leadership. Byeronov issued his orders for the attack on the building, stating that 'the secret of our action must be rigorously protected. Do not let any person leave the palace alive'. However, at first the president's guard put up stiff resistance, but the sheer savagery of the

Spetsnaz assault eventually overcame the defenders, and Amin and all but one of his guards were killed. As was Byeronov, killed by one of his own men by mistake. One of the Russians who took part in the assault later reported that 'the Spetsnaz used weapons equipped with silencers and shot down their adversaries like professional killers'.

Wars always spawn a host of irregular units, whose brief may include assassination missions. During the Vietnam War, for example, Captain Stanley Kraznoff of the Australian SAS organised a Mobile Guerrilla Force consisting of Green Berets, Australian SAS, Cambodians and US Rangers. Its tasks included operations in Cambodia assassinating North Vietnamese military personnel, along with the occasional capture of said personnel for intelligence purposes. The SEALs also made unofficial forays into Cambodia.

For these missions SEAL personnel would be dressed in Viet Cong (VC) 'black pyjamas' and head scarves. Under the Phoenix Program, the SEALs would liaise with so-called Provincial Reconnaissance Units (PRUs), groups of VC defectors organised in each province under South Vietnamese police control, whose job was to provide accurate information on the location of key VC personnel, who could then be eradicated.

The SEALs went in quick and got out fast. A SEAL commander, Lieutenant Yaw, describes a mission against a VC battalion command post outside Saigon: 'I got my pistol, walked over to the main bed, lifted the mosquito net and shot two guys in the head. Blood and brain matter splattered everywhere as [Chief Petty Officer] Gallagher hosed down a bunch with his M16. A VC leaping from another bed tried to push me as he made for his AK, but I punched him in

Above: Members of the Mobile Guerrilla Force with captured North Vietnamese weapons during the Vietnam War. This irregular unit, made up of US Green Berets, Rangers, Australian SAS and Cambodians, assassinated North Vietnamese personnel in Cambodia.

the face before he could grab his weapon and shot him.' Yaw and two others were then wounded by a grenade going off, so they called in helicopter evacuation. As they made their way to the rendezvous they 'got to a hooch. There were five Vietnamese inside and we were in no mood to ask questions. Having to assume they were VC, we shot them.' Such actions may appear harsh, but as another Vietnam SEAL stated: 'Our attitude was "If you fuck with us, we'll blow you away". But then again, you know, it was a business, and the business was terrorism.'

Working in conjunction with the PRUs, SEALs ambushed and killed VC tax collectors, most notably in the Rung Sat Special Zone south of Saigon, nicknamed the 'Forest of Assassins'. To carry out their tasks the SEALs were equipped with heavy firepower. A typical three-man SEAL team would be armed with an Ithaca M37 12-gauge fighting shotgun, M16 assault rifle with M203 grenade launcher attached and a Stoner M63A1 light machine gun. The latter had one basic mechanism, into which could be fitted various barrels, stocks and magazines. It was usually fed from a plastic magazine, although the SEALs favoured a 150-round box magazine, which gave them a light weapon capable of laying down sustained fire in continuous bursts. It did have its drawbacks, though. First, because it was gas fed it required a great deal of maintenance, and in less experienced hands it had a nasty tendency to malfunction and fire full-automatic without warning.

The 'Hush Puppy'

Another weapon favoured by SEAL assassin teams in Vietnam was the Smith and Wesson Mk 22, Model O 9mm handgun. Nicknamed the 'Hush Puppy' on account of it being used to kill enemy guard dogs, it was specially designed for the SEALs by Smith and Wesson. Based on the Model 39 pistol, it was equipped with a 127mm (5in) threaded barrel, to which could be attached a silencer. To make the weapon ever quieter, the slide could be locked, thereby keeping the mecha-nism closed and silent when firing. The 9mm round is normally supersonic, which creates an audible crack when fired, so a sub-sonic round was developed for the 'Hush Puppy' to eliminate this. The resultant green-tipped Parabellum round had a reduced muzzle velocity of 274mps (890fps), and the pistol was also equipped with special caps and plugs to allow it to be carried underwater. The ammunition was packed in boxes holding 22 rounds and a spare insert for the suppressor. Each insert would last around 30 rounds before having to be replaced.

French Assassins

The French have their own unit capable of carrying out selective assassination. This is *29ème Service de Action* (29 SA), the secret operations branch of French military intelligence, the *Direction Générale de Securité de L'Etat* (DGSE). Among the missions carried out by 29 SA are those in Lebanon, especially the retaliatory assassinations of terrorists involved in the September 1981 assassination of Louis Delamère, the French Ambassador in Beirut. The 20 or so 29 SA members travelled separately to Beirut; once there they organised into a basic intelligence team, an information-gathering team and an action team. The intelligence collected led to the assumption of Syrian involvement. A member of the intelligence team sets out the next step: 'so we concentrated on finding people, mainly young Arab Moslems, who had been rejected or were dissatisfied with some of the Syrian-backed terrorist organisations operating in Lebanon. With their help we were able to plant penetration agents in some of the groups and manipulate them.' After eight months of painstaking work, the trail led to the Bekaa Valley, and then to a Syrian-paid assassin named Sadek Mousawi. The French operatives were able to determine that Mousawi and another gunman, Muhammad Yacine, were the assassins, with another three or four acting in support.

The information was relayed to the action team, who laid their plans. On a June 1982

morning, Mousawi, Yacine and another terrorist were ambushed in their Mercedes car by two unmarked cars carrying 29 SA operatives. They stopped the terrorists' car and then sprayed it at close range with submachine-gun fire. Yacine and the third man were killed, though Mousawi was only wounded. However, the French team finished the job one week later when two 29 SA men disguised as hospital staff entered the Beirut hospital where Mousawi was recovering, and shot him dead in his bed.

Another French unit that specialises in termination is GIGN. In January 1985, for example, GIGN snipers had stalked the leaders of the nationalist Kanak movement in the equatorial jungle of New Caledonia (under French administration, New Caledonia contains three main racial groups, the indigenous Kanaks, in the majority until the 1960s but now in the minority, settlers from Polynesia and Asia, and Europeans; there are

racial tensions between the Europeans and Kanaks, not least because of the former mistreatment of the latter by the former). The GIGN team, under the command of Captain Denis Favier, took up positions some 250m (810ft) from a small farmhouse in the middle of a jungle clearing. Sitting on the floor of the small entrance porch was Eloi Machoro, 'minister of internal security' of the *Front de Libération Nationale Kanak Socialist*, along with two others. Two sentries with shotguns patrolled nearby. The four GIGN snipers were then ordered to open fire. Two snipers shot Machoro and another Kanak respectively, while a third sniper killed the other man on the porch and then a nearby sentry. The other sentry was killed by the fourth sniper. The remarks of Captain Favier after the operation give a clue as to those who authorise elite teams to carry out assassinations: 'the decision to fire was very quick; it was a political decision'.

Above: Russia's Spetsnaz includes assassination in its wartime and peacetime roles.

CHAPTER 12

INFILTRATION

Insertion techniques are an essential part of special forces missions. Being able to infiltrate unseen into enemy territory, by land, sea or air, is crucial to the success of teams which operate behind the lines. To support infiltration, elite units can call upon a plethora of sophisticated hardware.

One of the problems associated with special forces operations is that of inserting teams into enemy territory. Once behind the lines, a small-sized elite unit can achieve results and inflict damage out of all proportion to its size, but it is worthless if it cannot be inserted covertly in the first place. This being the case, armed forces around the world have devoted much time and resources to finding the best ways of getting their personnel into and out of the war zone without detection. This chapter will examine the ways special forces teams enter enemy territory by air, sea and land.

Parachuting is a skill traditionally associated with special forces, and most elite units, such as the British, New Zealand and Australian SAS, US Navy SEALs, US Green Berets, US Rangers and a host of other formations, train their members in parachute techniques. At the very least this involves training personnel to conduct static-line drops, whereby a large number of troops will exit transport aircraft and their parachutes will open automatically. This sort of drop is now used on the battlefield to block an enemy advance, to hold objectives immediately behind the lines or against a Third World power whose air defences are poor. A static-line drop requires total air superiority as the transports are very vulnerable to anti-aircraft defences and enemy aircraft. The troops will be dropped from a height of around 500m (1600ft), with each man carrying up to 70kg (150lb) of equipment in an equipment container, which, when the paratrooper is in the air, is released to hang below him on a suspension rope. This allows the soldier to perform a roll when landing to absorb the shock. The parachutes themselves

Left: US SEALs emerge from the surf after an underwater approach to a hostile beach. SEALs are also expert at airborne insertion techniques.

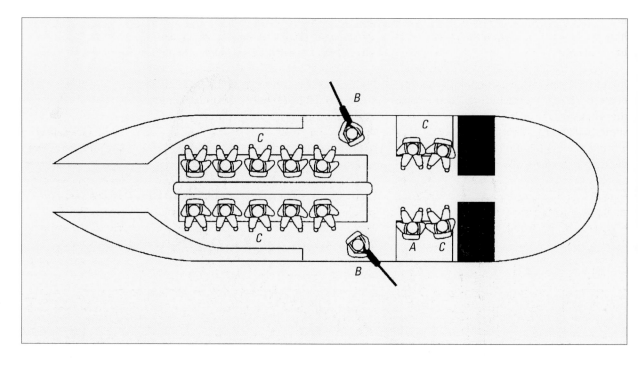

Above: The seating plan for an elite team being helicoptered into enemy territory (the aircraft has two side exit doors). The commander (A) is first out on landing, while the machine gunners (B) cover the exit of the team (C).

have poor manoeuvrability, which means wind can blow them off course. If this happens, organisation on the ground can suffer.

Examples of static-line drops in recent years include the American invasions of Grenada in 1983 and Panama in 1989. In both cases the Americans mustered overwhelming force against outnumbered and poorly organised defenders. However, the transports carrying US paratroopers had to proceed with extreme caution against even rudimentary anti-aircraft defences. During the invasion of Grenada, US Rangers were ordered to capture Point Salines Airport. The Rangers made the drop from MC-130 Combat Talon transport aircraft (special operations variants of the C-130 Lockheed Hercules), which approached the island low from the south to avoid radar detection. They were also escorted by gunships.

The defenders were taken by surprise, but still managed to put up such a barrage of fire that the Ranger commander, Lieutenant-Colonel Ralph Hagler, decided to abort the jump until the gunships had suppressed the anti-aircraft fire. Then the Rangers jumped.

Hagler and his men jumped from a minimum height with no reserve 'chutes (there would have been no time to deploy a second 'chute if the main one malfunctioned) with very heavy loads. In 21 seconds the 250 Rangers had exited the aircraft and landed on the airport tarmac. There was only one jump injury as the Rangers cleared the blocked runway for follow-on forces.

The Rangers fared less well during the December 1989 invasion of Panama. The 2nd Battalion, 75th Ranger Regiment, was dropped from C-130s as part of Task Force Red, whose job was to seize Rio Hato Military Base. They were dropped in the early hours of 19 December, having been preceded by two F-117 Stealth Fighters, which dropped two 900kg (2000lb) bombs to panic the defenders, though this served only to alert the Panamanians. The Rangers jumped from an altitude of 150m (500ft) into small-arms and anti-aircraft fire. There were 35 jump injuries, but this did not stop them seizing the base and blocking the nearby Inter-American Highway at a cost of four dead and 27 wounded. But both Grenada and Panama illustrate the high vulnerability of even highly trained troops when making a static-line parachute drop.

A more speedy and covert way of inserting elite troops by air is high altitude, low opening (HALO) parachuting. In this case the troops exit the aircraft at an altitude of some 10,000m (32,000ft), then freefall to an altitude of about 760m (2500ft), when they deploy their 'chutes. However, HALO parachuting requires a great deal of training. The freefaller, for example, has to maintain a stable position during his flight with a heavy bergen on his back and his weapon strapped to his body by a harness. The team must exit the aircraft together because advanced aerial

manoeuvres are impossible in the thin air above 6100m (20,000ft). Because of wind drift – 3m (10ft) for every 31m (100ft) of fall and every knot of wind – the team has to track in flight. This involves arching the body into a crude aerofoil to direct the windflow along its underside. The arms are swept back to lower the head and increase the rate of descent and horizontal movement.

At such altitudes the HALO jumper needs oxygen-breathing equipment to avoid hypoxia. He also needs a barometric trigger to activate his 'chute automatically at an altitude of 600m (2000ft). The soldier will usually deploy his own 'chute, but triggers such as the British Irvin Hitefinder D/1 Mk 4 act as

Below: Members of the British Parachute Regiment's Pathfinder Platoon conduct a high altitude, low opening (HALO) parachute descent. All are wearing oxygen-breathing kit.

safety devices by activating the parachute-release mechanism at the critical altitude of 600m (2000ft) (at this height the paratrooper still has time to deploy his reserve if the main parachute malfunctions). Apart from the parachute not opening, there are other dangers associated with parachuting from great heights. These include stress-induced hyperventilation, leading to a severe lowering of blood carbon dioxide and unconsciousness, barometric trauma (which results from air getting into the intestines, ears and sinuses and then expanding due to the lower air pressures at high altitudes). In addition, the paratrooper will be exposed to low temperatures due to the windchill factor as he freefalls. This may result in ice forming on his equipment, especially his goggles. These problems mean that HALO jumpers need to be in prime physical shape and highly skilled, both of which require a great deal of time and training. As a result, only the premier elite units train their men in HALO parachuting techniques, such as the SAS units, Delta Force, SEALs and the various pathfinder formations.

High altitude, high opening (HAHO) parachuting is another technique employed by special forces. It differs from HALO in that the paratrooper is dropped from the aircraft wearing oxygen-breathing equipment at an altitude of 10,000m (32,000ft), freefalls for 8-10 seconds then deploys his 'chute at around 8500m (27,600ft). He then makes a gradual descent to the ground – which can take between 70-80 minutes – by which time he will have travelled up to 30km (19 miles). This means the team can be dropped outside enemy territory, allowing them to drift into hostile airspace unseen by radar. But there are problems associated with HAHO parachuting. The team must stay together once the canopies are opened to be sure of landing together. The actual flight to the drop zone (DZ) requires pinpoint accuracy, as it will be invisible because HAHO drops are conducted at night. This means wearing chest-pack Global Positioning System (GPS) sets. This allows the paratrooper to check his position via up to 100 waypoints between his release point and the DZ.

Specialist Parachutes

HAHO and HALO parachute techniques require specialist parachutes. Units such as the British SAS use the GQ 360 nine-cell flat ramair canopy, which has the same aerodynamic properties as an aircraft wing. In addition, the parachutes will have panels coated with a luminous material that emits a dull glow, which allows the team to stick together and mitigates against mid-air collisions. But

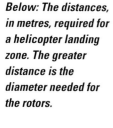

Below: The distances, in metres, required for a helicopter landing zone. The greater distance is the diameter needed for the rotors.

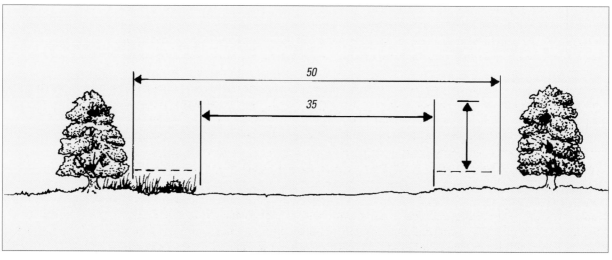

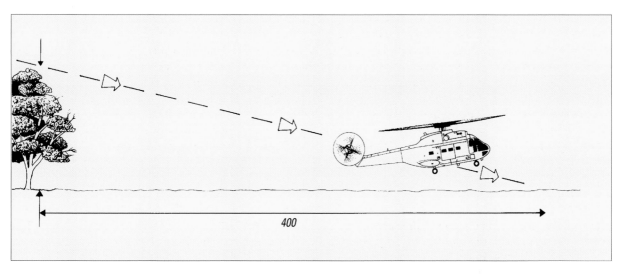

400

it is not only in the air that problems can occur. During the aforementioned American invasion of Grenada, SEAL and Delta Force personnel made HALO descents onto the island the night before the invasion took place to rescue certain individuals and put Radio Free Grenada out of action. However, one of the aircraft transporting the troops experienced an equipment failure and over-shot the DZ, dropping some paratroopers into the sea. Four SEALs became entangled in their parachutes on landing in the water and drowned.

Rough Airstrips

A way around the problem of parachuting elite teams is to land aircraft on runways and simply offload the occupants. During World War II, for example, British SAS teams in France after D-Day sometimes made use of the single-engined Lysander to evacuate wounded personnel, agents or downed Allied airmen. Aircraft such as the Lysander require an airstrip at least 92m (300ft) long, but heavier transports need runways at least 370m (1200ft) to land and take off safely. If an established runway is not available, a rough strip will have to be built. Ideally elite teams arrive and leave during darkness, thus the airstrip will need some sort of illumination or beacon system to guide in the pilot.

During the Vietnam War, for example, the Central Intelligence Agency (CIA) built a series of landing strips to support its private army in Laos. In World War II, SAS teams in Europe used the Eureka beacon to guide air-craft in. An open field about 900m (2900ft) long would be selected and three red lights placed 100m (320ft) apart in the middle of the field. A fourth, white light would be placed 45m (150ft) to the right of the last red light, which meant the lights were in an L-shaped formation. The white light flashed Morse recognition signals when the aircraft arrived overhead. The latter approached the DZ at an altitude of 200m (650ft), and dropped its load when it was over the second red light.

Once on the ground, be it by parachute or leaving an aircraft on the ground, the team leader will gather together his men. Each member of the team will have memorised the location of the rendezvous (RV) point and emergency RVs. To assist in gathering the team, the commander will activate a portable radio homing beacon which emits a weak, high-frequency signal. When the other team members land they activate their personal hand-held radio receivers, which pick up the commander's signals and convert them into an audible bleep. The signal becomes stronger when the radio receiver is pointed

Above: The minimum distance, in metres, required for a helicopter to touch down.

Right: Immediately upon landing, the elite team will exit as quickly as possible and assume an all-round defence. The machine gun teams (A) are first on the ground. The team commander (B) and second-in-command (C) separate in order to reduce the chances of them both being killed.

directly at the beacon, which leads the team to the commander.

If the DZ is 'hot', the team members will deploy for contact and begin laying down a barrage of small-arms fire. This will allow the commander to request an immediate extraction or shoot his way out of the contact. More likely, though, the team will have landed undetected, and the DZ will have to be sterilised. This means recovering all parachute equipment and burying it. All caches have to be concealed and their position carefully noted. Nothing should be left which will indicate to the enemy that a special forces team has landed.

Despite the parachute training given to elite troops, parachute insertion is being downgraded as a method of insertion. Special forces troops will continue to receive para training during their careers (it is one way of determining whether individuals have the 'right stuff' to be elite soldiers), but helicopter insertion is now the primary aerial delivery method for specialist teams. Unsurprisingly, it is the United States which leads the way with regard to helicopter technology. The 1st Air Force Special Operations Wing was initially equipped with 40 Sikorsky MH-53J Pave Low III helicopters. This remarkable aircraft was a variant of the Sikorsky Sea Stallion. It was equipped with night vision sensors, electronic countermeasures (ECM) and an aerial refuelling probe. It has been replaced by the HH-60 Night Hawk, a variant of the UH-60 Black Hawk. The Night Hawk has avionics similar to those of the Pave Low

III, plus doppler navigation radar, a forward-looking infrared sensor and a more comprehensive ECM suite. The advantage of helicopters fitted with these systems is that they can fly at treetop level in what is known as nap-of-the-earth (NOE) flying. This is used by helicopters for maximum terrain cover and requires careful route planning to avoid hills and ridge lines. Because of the dangers involved with NOE, helicopters usually fly at a speed of no greater than 140kph (90mph). At such speeds helicopters can be flown manually by pilots wearing night vision goggles, whereas fixed-wing aircraft flying at low levels employ an autopilot directed by a terrain-following radar to avoid obstacles. Night Hawks are used by American elite teams, but they also make use of the larger CH-47 Chinook transport helicopter to get them to the target. Able to carry up to 44 fully equipped troops, the latest Chinooks are equipped with all-weather instrumentation and full ECM suite. During the 1991 Gulf War, for example, SAS road watch patrols were inserted into Iraq by RAF Chinooks. One of the pilots who flew Chinooks in support of SAS operations describes flying NOE thus: 'Putting it down at night, seeing through NVGs, is the main trick we have to learn. In Saudi Arabia, it's normal for the pilots to lose complete sight of the ground from 50ft [15m] altitudes due to sand clouds. It was almost a relief when we got into Iraq because the ground was more solid than the chalk dust of the Saudi desert, which was the worst thing about flying there.'

Helicopter DZs

Flying at such altitudes means running the risk of being hit by enemy ground fire, especially from troops. The pilot then has to get lower, as the same RAF pilot states: 'It takes you out of their arc of fire in a lot less time than ascending, which runs the additional risk of getting you locked into an enemy SAM [Surface-to-Air Missile] radar'.

Once the helicopter arrives at the DZ, the team must exit the aircraft as quickly as pos-

sible, which means throwing packs out of the doors and assuming an all-round defence. Normally the helicopter will touch down, but in long grass or uneven terrain it will hover at around 2m (6ft), which means the men will have to jump to the ground. When being picked up, the team should enter the aircraft in the reverse order that they left the aircraft. When getting back on board all team members should ensure that their personal weapons have empty breeches and safety catches applied to guard against accidental discharges in the fuselage. Bergens and other items of equipment should have been thrown into the helicopter beforehand, though with models such as the Puma and Black Hawk, which have doors either side of

Below: Helicopter emplaning procedure after a mission. The team divides into two files and enters via the side doors once the aircraft touches down.

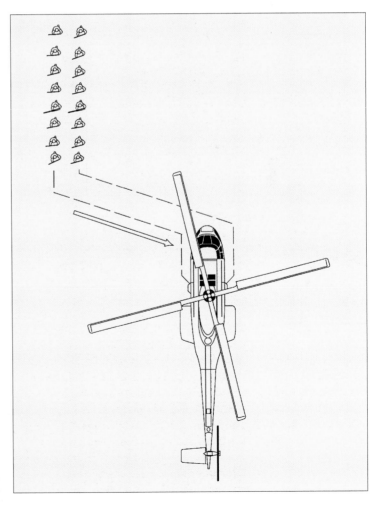

145

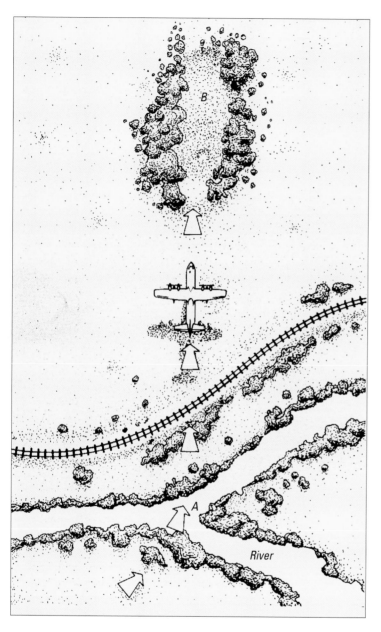

Above: Re-supply operations for elite teams are aided by providing pilots with landmarks. Aircraft are always given an initial point (A) and the drop zone (B).

use of underwater breathing equipment. Teams using scuba equipment can infiltrate harbours and rivers either to move farther inland or carry out sabotage missions against shipping or coastal targets. To do so, elite units such as the US Navy's SEALs and British Special Boat Service (SBS) use closed-circuit rebreather equipment, which does not produce a cloud of bubbles from expired air. Instead, the rebreather removes exhaled carbon dioxide and recharges the remaining nitrogen with pulsed oxygen. This means that a 0.34 cubic-metre (12.7cubic-foot) cylinder lasts for around four hours. But with this kit divers can only dive to a depth of 9m (30ft), because pure oxygen becomes toxic at pressures over two atmospheres. Each diver will also have to carry his equipment and explosives, often limpet mines. Each mine can weigh up to 15kg (33lb), and though constructed of synthetic material to aid buoyancy, mines are still a substantial load to carry. Due to the stresses involved in military diving and the equipment loads to be carried, the maximum distance for a combat swim is around 1.5km (0.9km). Among the most popular rebreather rigs are the Oxymax and Drager Lar V.

Subskimmers

Because of the taxing nature of swimming to the target, many elite units use swimmer delivery vehicles to transport teams to the target. A recent innovation is the so-called subskimmer, which is a semi-inflatable 'boat' that can travel on the surface and underwater. The actual conversion to submarine is simple: the pilot seals off the engine and instrument compartment and then deflates the side tubes. For an approach to the target it is possible to adopt a snorkel mode, whereby only the air inlet, exhaust pipes and divers' heads are visible on the surface. This is probably the best mode because it is extremely difficult for the naked eye to spot and offers a low radar profile. The subskimmer can also approach the target underwater, powered by two electric motors. And the

the fuselage, care must be taken that kit thrown forcefully in one side does not fly out the door opposite! The team leader should confirm that everyone is safely aboard before telling the pilot to take off.

Rivers and coastlines offer special forces units another way of covertly infiltrating enemy territory, but waterborne operations require troops who are highly trained in the crew can leave it 'parked' on the sea bed while they carry out their mission. The British Submersible Recovery Craft (SRC) is powered by twin outboard motors and can cruise on the surface at a speed of 30-45 knots, while below the waves, propelled by electric motors, its speed is 2-3 knots.

The SEALs use the Mark 8 Swimmer Delivery Vehicle (SDV), which can carry six soldiers. It is 9m (30ft) long and 90cm (3ft) wide, having a torpedo-like shape. Powered by electric motors, the SDV can maintain an underwater speed of 3-4 knots for several hours. However, the men sit astride the SDV in their wet suits and their breathing equipment in a crouched posture that is very physically demanding. This means they have to rest onshore for several hours after their journey to recuperate. If the SEALs have left the SDV on the sea bed, they can locate it by means of an underwater beacon. If they have been dropped off initially by submarine, they can find their way back via a second beacon dropped by the submarine at a pre-arranged rendezvous. A third beacon, on the submarine itself and transmitting on a different frequency, guides the SDV in.

Boats and Dinghies

Surface craft offer a quicker way of getting special forces teams onto a shore or riverbank. However, there are attendant dangers involved with small boats. They have little protection and, if spotted, can be blown out of the water with relative ease. Outboard motors are noisy, but if the team decides to uses oars or paddles this will substantially increase the amount of time on the water. Nevertheless, small boats do have several advantages with regard to inserting teams: they can transport large quantities of weapons and equipment and provide access to areas that are impenetrable to foot patrols, such as dense jungle.

Typical vessels used by elite teams for infiltration include the British Rigid Raider, a small, fast craft used by units such as the SAS, SBS and Royal Marines for amphibious

operations. It is capable of carrying up to nine fully equipped troops at speeds up to 40 knots. Then there is a range of inflatable boats, which can carry up to 12 soldiers and are powered by outboard motors. On a river mission, if there are two or more boats, additional security can be provided by using the so-called 'alternative bounds' tactic. One boat stops and its crew keep watch on the river ahead. The second boat, covered by the team on the bank, then moves forward to establish an observation position on the opposite bank, and so on. Another tactic is moving up a river in successive bounds, which involves having a dedicated scout vessel moving forward in successive bounds while all the time being covered by the other boats.

Above: Powered inflatable dinghies are ideal for the speedy insertion of heavily laden elite teams, though they are noisy and vulnerable to attack.

Elite units have always made use of vehicles to infiltrate teams on land. During World War II, for example, British SAS units used Willys Jeeps and a range of trucks to transport teams to and from targets in the vast wastes of North Africa. This tradition was continued in the deserts of Iraq during the 1991 Gulf War, when SAS fighting columns mounted on heavily armed Land Rover 110 vehicles roamed behind enemy lines hunting for mobile Scud surface-to-surface missile launchers. The Land Rovers were armed with a combination of Browning heavy machine guns, GPMGs, Mark 19 grenade launchers, Milan anti-tank missiles and Stinger surface-to-air missiles.

The Australian SAS also favours Land Rover vehicles, as they are ideal for coping with the long distances involved in operations in the vastness of the Northern Territory and Western Australia. Units such as the US Green Berets, SEALs and Delta Force use the High Mobility Multi-Purpose Wheeled Vehicle (HMMWV), which is designed to operate in all types of terrain and weather conditions. Vehicles which pack more punch are employed by the cavalry regiments of the French Foreign Legion. These include the AMX-10RC tank destroyer, which can knock out other armoured vehicles with its 105mm main gun. Such vehicles are potent in the offensive, but are vulnerable to faster-moving vehicles armed with anti-armour weapons, and to ground troops equipped with similar hardware. Whatever vehicles are being used, elite teams favour the hours of darkness for vehicle travel. This reduces the chances of convoys being spotted, especially by enemy aircraft.

Insertion over land using vehicles is not the only way elite teams can infiltrate enemy territory. Literally walking across borders is another means, though of course highly defended borders offer major obstacles. Modern borders can be guarded by a plethora of defences, such as infrared cameras and microwave beams. Beyond these electronic defences can be found watchtowers manned by guards, plus ditches filled with anti-personnel mines and barbed wire. Even darkness offers little cover, as the enemy can employ image intensifiers and thermal imagers. It is because of these defences that special forces teams favour aerial or water-

Right: A Land Rover 110 vehicle, ideal for long-range land infiltration. Note the sand channel, three GPMGs and smoke dischargers on the front and rear bumpers.

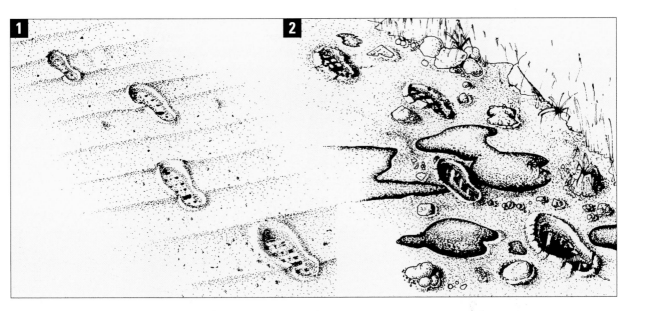

borne insertion as a way of getting into hostile territory.

Whatever method of insertion is used by an elite team, each member of the group will be fully trained in evasion techniques. Being able to get back to friendly territory in the event that exfiltration is unavailable is integral to being a special forces soldier. As the US Army's escape and evasion manual states: 'You become an evader when isolated in hostile areas, are unable to continue the assigned mission, and are prevented from rejoining your unit ... The situation must be evaluated and a plan of action prepared before leaving the initial hiding place.'

The general principles of evasion are simple. They include avoiding major roads and populated areas and making full use of camouflage and concealment. The latter is particularly important, and involves employing the natural concealment afforded by darkness, wooded terrain and general foliage. Travel must be conducted at night, the ground to be travelled over having previously been studied during daylight hours. When travelling, the evader will come across streams and rivers. These will have to be forded, as bridges and ferries will be guarded. Ridge lines can be fatal to evaders, and each

member of the team must stay well below the summit to avoid being silhouetted against the skyline.

In general, teams will attempt to evade by splitting into groups of not more than four men, with one man in command of each group. This reduces the chances of detection, improves movement and control and creates a more tightly-knit group.

All the above sounds fairly straightforward, but evasion calls upon all the strength, tenacity and mental ability of elite troops. Sometimes these qualities are not enough. During the 1991 Gulf War, for example, a British eight-man SAS team, codenamed 'Bravo Two Zero', was inserted behind Iraqi lines to watch for mobile Scud launchers. Inserted by Chinook helicopter, the team was soon discovered by the Iraqis and forced to seek the safety of Syria. However, the SAS team had to battle against the weather as well as the pursuing Iraqis, and soon they took losses. One, Sergeant Vince Phillips, became isolated and died of hypothermia. Four were captured and another two, Trooper Robert Consiglio and Lance-Corporal 'Legs' Lane, were killed by enemy gunfire. Only one man made it to Syria: Chris Ryan, who walked 300km (190 miles) to reach safety.

Above: Successful evasion means not leaving footprints in sand (1) or mud (2), which act as signposts to the enemy.

CHAPTER 13

NIGHT FIGHTING

Night fighting tactics must be mastered by elite soldiers to 'own the night'. This means learning how to shoot correctly in darkness, specialist movement techniques and drills for fighting in low-light conditions with edged weapons. Above all, it means making use of all the human senses.

The night is the friend of special forces units. It allows teams to infiltrate and move unseen through and across front lines, and it provides cover for a rapid withdrawal. But operating in darkness requires special training and preparation, for night fighting puts unique physical and psychological strains upon the human body.

The first problem that must be overcome at night is limited vision. Human beings can see at night thanks to special cells in the eyes called rods. These rods require at least 30 minutes of acclimatisation to activate, and they can be 'burnt out' when exposed to light. In addition, excessive sunlight will degrade night vision for around 36 hours, thus elite troops operating in high sunlight conditions, such as in the desert, will wear sunglasses during the day if operating at night. The eyes also have problems estimating distance at night. Small objects, for example, seem farther away and larger objects closer, as the brain judges distances partly by size relationships. By way of compensation, though, hearing becomes more acute at night because of lower background noise, and cold, moist air carries sound better. Using hearing at night requires much training so the soldier can discriminate multiple sounds and faint sounds. A rifle bolt closing, for example, can be heard from a great distance.

Left: Soldiers patrolling at night. The one on the right is wearing night vision goggles, which allow the wearer to see clearly in the dark.

The sense of smell can also be utilised at night. One of the training aids used by elite troops to take advantage of smell at night is for a soldier to face 45 degrees towards the wind, relax and breathe normally but take sharp, frequent sniffs. In this way he can discern different smells which may give clues as to the presence of an enemy.

Elite teams operating at night need to take account of the problem of fatigue. This can be overcome by implementing a number of tactical procedures. These include having an on-off schedule so everyone gets some rest, scheduling meal breaks so that everyone is at optimum efficiency. Carbohydrates, for example, require at least 30 minutes to reach the blood stream; this needs to be taken into account by commanders planning actions or advances. Fatigued soldiers are a liability at night, as they do not think clearly. Commanders therefore must try and ensure they get some rest and food.

Silent movement at night is essential for special forces missions. Training emphasises moving slowly with small, high steps, feeling carefully before shifting the weight onto the leading foot, while at the same time scanning ahead. Troops moving in file must try to step in the footsteps of the leading soldier as those spaces will have already been cleared

Right: A night firing exercise. At night all soldiers have a tendency to shoot high because they look at the centre of the target when firing. Only regular night firing can remedy this.

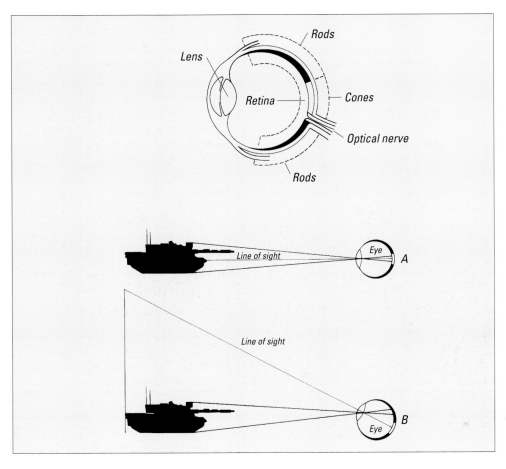

Left: The rods of the human eye are very sensitive to light. In daylight (A), to see the target the viewer has to look at it. At night, the cone cells will not register the target. By looking away, the target will be visible as any light hits the rods (B).

of obstacles. This tactic will not only help silent movement, it will also deceive the enemy as to the size of the unit. All branches and bushes should be carefully pushed aside when moving and then replaced. If they are broken they will leave white spots on the sides of trees or shrubs – these are very visible at night.

When moving during the day soldiers thrust their feet well forward, straightening a leg before the heel hits the ground. Then the weight of the body is pushed forward and the rear foot is swung forward, using the calf muscles to move the body forward. At night, however, troops use their thigh and buttock muscles to move. The individual slowly lifts his left leg to nearly knee height, balancing on his right, and then eases it forward, while at the same time feeling for trip wires and

twigs. The toe is pointed down and used to feel the ground with the outside of the toe of the boot. If all is clear, the toe is settled on the ground, then the heel, all the time feeling for loose rocks or twigs. When he is confident of a solid footing, he slowly rolls his weight forward and then, following a slight pause, begins to right his left boot.

Another tactic used at night when moving is the stalk. This is done when approaching a sentry, for example. The stalk is essentially walking at night, very slowly, in a crouch. Often the stalk is made by crawling, since looking from low to high is more effective and a crawling soldier has a lower silhouette. The fastest crawl is made by pressing the arm and foot on the same side of the body against the ground to pull or push forward. This method can be rather noisy; a quieter way involves pressing down an arm and a foot on opposite sides and resting on one hip. An even quieter method of crawling involves using the toes and elbows to lift and move the torso forward slowly. When crawling, the soldier feels for twigs and rocks and either removes them or goes round them.

Because of the lack of light, navigation at night is more difficult, but it uses the same two basic methods as day navigation. These are terrain association, which uses a general direction of travel and the recognition of terrain features on both the map and the ground, and dead reckoning, which uses a compass direction and specific distance. When using terrain association, the soldier studies the features around him and orients the map to the terrain. This allows him mentally to picture the landforms and their silhouettes as seen from his location, determine the direction of each landform and its relative steepness in his vicinity, identify high ground and other key terrain, identify the avenues of approach towards key terrain features, and determine what the skyline looks like in any direction from a specified location in his area of operation.

Terrain Analysis

Terrain analysis involves carrying out a reconnaissance of the ground, looking at the map and confirming or modifying perceptions about its appearance. An essential part of this for the elite trooper is forming a mental picture and then modifying it section by section. Terrain analysis involves determining which way the rivers run, which features will be seen at night and the positioning of fences and other man-made features. In terrain such as dense jungle, where the only thing to be seen is trees, an elite soldier will have to use his compass to navigate, which will mean literally holding it in front of him and following the compass bearing (the compass pointer will be luminous to aid him).

Dead reckoning involves a soldier plotting and recording a series of courses before he sets out, each one being measured in terms of distance and direction between two points. These courses lead from the starting point to his final destination, and they enable him to determine his position at any time, either by following his plan or by comparing his actual position on the ground in relation to his plotted course. Navigating by dead reckoning requires a map to select and plot a route, a compass for direction finding, a protractor for plotting direction and distance on the map, and a route card and log.

The Route Card

Having determined his starting point and plotted his route on a map, an elite soldier will make out his route card, which describes each leg of the proposed route in terms of distance and direction. When he has completed his route card he is ready to move. When moving, he must keep a careful record of each bearing taken and the distance covered on each bearing, and if he deviates from his route must make adjustments to his route and record them in the log. If he is operating in an area where contact with the enemy is likely, he will not write anything down, as this information may be useful to an enemy if he is captured.

Knowing as much as possible about the enemy will aid an elite team operating at night. This involves knowing his operational techniques and studying his positions during reconnaissance patrols. A careless enemy will leave telltale signs of his presence, which can then be used against him. Moved stones, crumbled ones, or those pressed into the earth; bushes or grasses bent, are all signs that an enemy patrol has been in the area. Stains are another give away. These may include blood, water on stones and crushed leaves. Active infrared devices may also be useful. Infrared sights work by the emission of beams in the infrared wavelength which illuminate the target (infrared radiation is emitted by all objects warmer than absolute zero – minus 273 degrees Centigrade). When viewed through infrared sights, broken and crushed vegetation gives a different signature to growing bushes, and newly dropped blood on bushes can also be identified.

Dropped litter is an example of the presence of ill-disciplined soldiers, though booby traps my have been left among the litter to kill the unwary. Sounds are also a give-away as to the location of the enemy. A soldier can place his ear on the ground or on a stick driven 150mm (6in) into the ground. It is hard to determine direction, but sounds can be heard from a long distance because the ground is denser than air and carries sound waves more efficiently. In addition, in light mist sounds will carry farther, though they can be masked by rain or wind. Rain may also cause soldiers to miss sounds due to hoods or caps – it is often worth having a wet head in order to hear telltale sounds. During a night approach all the team should be hatless, and especially devoid of helmets. Helmets make hollow sounds in the rain, whistle during breezes and generally rattle and rustle, masking important sounds.

Poor enemy camouflage can also be a signpost to an attacking team. In particular, team members should look for straight lines (rarely found in nature), contrasts in colour or tone and unnatural vegetation, such as green leaves among dead branches. Having detected the enemy, a team must determine the distance to the opposition's unit. This can be far from easy, as judging distances depends on individuals' ability and the amount of water vapour in the air. Clear, dry desert air, for example, allows an individual to detect sights at a greater distance, but does not carry sound or odours as well as more humid air. Sounds can be a real problem with regard to estimating distances, as they can bounce among buildings and rocky terrain and mislead an individual as to the direction of their source. Sound travels at around 300m (1000ft) per second, so the elite soldier should count the seconds between seeing the flash of a weapon firing and hearing its report. The number of seconds multiplied by three equates to the distance to the weapon in hundreds of metres.

Night fighting requires much training and practice, especially with regard to shooting. In general, soldiers have a tendency to shoot

Below: All team members must take care when moving in low-light conditions. These men have allowed themselves to be silhouetted – giving their location away to the enemy.

Below: The view through a thermal imaging scope at night. Note the armoured vehicle in the centre.

high at night. This is because they tend to look at the centre of the target when firing. To remedy this entails concentrating on the base of the target with their dominant eye. In addition, the shooter should fire as soon as the rifle is pointed at the target, with a sharp pull on the trigger. If he uses a steady squeeze he will disrupt his concentration and the weapon's alignment. One way of ensuring that the muzzle is depressed when the weapon fires is to stare at a spot, close the

eyes and then attempt to point at the spot, first with the finger and then with the rifle. In this way an individual develops a 'feel' for pointing his rifle (moving the hand forward on the stock often corrects a tendency for aiming high). Focusing the centre of the eye on a target at night causes the target to disappear because of the scarcity of night vision cells in the centre of the eye.

Precisely identifying targets at night may be difficult, especially when individuals

Left: A sock wrapped around a grenade, slit and then folded back on itself and tied under the main body can be used as a throwing aid by acting as a sling. It improves accuracy.

cannot use terrain features as points of reference. In the defence, therefore, a commander may put reflective or luminous marks on trees or rocks in assigned sectors. The height of the spots will be known to each member of the team, which will facilitate aiming low and effectively. Each member of the team will have also memorised the area in front of him so he can picture it at night (the luminous dots will help him keep track of where features are). If an enemy approach is heard, each man will be able to fire directly at targets even without seeing them. If footsteps are heard in dry bushes, for example, a soldier will be able to picture the area and know where they lie in relation to his position.

When it comes to actual night fighting, some weapons are more effective than others. Rifles and machine guns equipped with night vision devices, for example, enable shooters to spot their targets. Mention

has already been made of infrared sights, but image intensifying sights are another way of seeing in the dark. These sights operate by amplifying low levels of visible light up to 100,000 times to produce a viewable image even on the darkest night. The dim light reflected by objects is collected by a lens and focused on a photo-cathode, which releases electrons when it absorbs photons of light. The electrons are then accelerated by an electrical field, which raises their energy levels, and projected onto a phosphor screen to generate a bright image. An alternative method of achieving higher light gain, channel electron amplification, relies on tubes lined with semi-conductor glass, formed into fibreoptic mosaics and inserted between a photo-cathode and a phosphor screen. Electrons generated by the photo-cathode collide with the semi-conductor tubes, releasing additional electrons, which are accelerated by an electrical field and projected onto the phosphor screen. Because of their light weight and low power requirements, image intensifiers are often mounted on rifles and machine guns, as well as being used for personal surveillance devices. They also have the advantage that they emit no radiation themselves, and are undetectable by an adversary. However, because they operate only in the visible spectrum, their effectiveness is degraded by smoke, dense foliage, fog and heavy precipitation. Laser sights are another means of seeing at night. They require the soldier to wear night vision goggles, which can discern an otherwise invisible beam emitted from a weapon mounting a laser aiming device. A more sophisticated device is the thermal imager (TI), which operates rather like a television camera but creates a picture using infrared 'heat' differences instead of light. A TI system can see men or machines through smoke, foliage or camouflage, by day or by night. They tend to be expensive and relatively fragile, and are usually found only on vehicles and heavy weapons, or as specialist observation devices.

Night Fighting Hand Grenades

At the other end of the sophistication scale, hand grenades can be effective weapons at night. They do not reveal a team's location, and even if they miss the target they can still stun and surprise an enemy force. When throwing grenades, though, team members must be careful with regard to overhead obstacles: no one wants to bounce a grenade back into his own position! At night grenades will therefore mostly be thrown underhand.

A sling adds leverage to hand grenades, increasing their range and accuracy. One way to do this is to fasten a cord around 0.75m (2ft) long to the grenade, release the pin, wait one second and then swing it towards the target. One twirl is enough to give the grenade maximum speed. To achieve the best results using this method, the grenade can be placed in the toe of a sock, with the cord then tied around the body

tightly near the neck. The sock is then split to let the cord hang out while the sock is folded down over the tie, away from the neck. The sock is then tied a second time tightly below the first tie, farther away from the handle.

Bayonet Fighting

Another crude but effective night fighting weapon is the bayonet. A US Special Forces night fighting manual has the following to say about this edged weapon: 'Bayonets are especially effective in night fighting. They are silent, adding confusion and intimidation to your arsenal; they are effective in close-quarter fighting; and they provide a psychological advantage because bayonet fighters are universally feared.' In addition to the problems associated with judging distance when fighting with a bayonet at night, there are psychological difficulties. The Special Forces manual again: 'new soldiers hesitate before attacking. Train night fighters to instantaneously lunge toward anyone who enters their position unannounced or toward any unidentified figure in the area. It is not necessary to get into a proper stance; that is, to check hand position, breathe, look hard, then lunge. That's too slow. Just lunge!'

Occasionally illumination will be employed during night operations. During the 1982 Falklands War, for example, the British Parachute Regiment's attack on Mount Longdon during the night of 11/12 June was successful mainly because of the excellent fighting quality of the British Paras. However, another factor was the neutralisation of Argentinian night vision devices by fire and artificial light at critical times. However, a commander using illumination will have to ask himself several questions: is the weather favourable, are illumination assets sufficient to support the operation, and what is the illumination being used for – reconnaissance, to aid an attack or to illuminate terrain features? Whatever the reasons, illumination has to be properly used. Light should silhouette targets, for example,

Left: Most special forces operations are conducted at night. Troops are therefore well trained in night fighting infiltration and fighting techniques.

instead of lighting them uniformly because uniform, or flat, light reduces contrast and make targets harder to see. A flare over a route may even aid the enemy by silhouetting friendly forces as they cross a ridge. This means routes towards the target must be planned carefully. Uppermost in a commander's mind will be the main considerations regarding illumination. First, overhead lighting, such as mortar or aircraft flares, is flat and of short duration, but it illuminates defilades. Second, angled lighting, such as from a searchlight or a flare over an adjacent area, shadows defilades but emphasises relief

and makes target recognition easier. The commander will also have to take into consideration the means of illumination at his disposal. An 81mm mortar illumination round, for example, lasts for around 75 seconds, has a maximum range of 3300m (10,700ft) and illuminates an area with a diameter of 1100m (3575ft). An illumination round fired from a 155mm howitzer, on the other hand, lasts for up to 150 seconds, has a range of up to 14km (8.7 miles) and illuminates an area with a diameter of 2000m (6500ft). However, illumination is only a small part of elite units 'owning the night'.

CHAPTER 14

TAKING ON AIRBORNE & ARMOURED PURSUERS

Aircraft and armoured vehicles pose a major threat to small-sized elite teams operating behind enemy lines, especially on foot. However, special forces soldiers are trained to deal with such threats, and have access to light but powerful anti-aircraft and anti-tank weapons to help them defeat the threat.

E lite teams are invariably lightly armed on operations. Whether they are mounted on vehicles, boats or devoid of any means of transport, they are very vulnerable to attack by enemy armour and aircraft. This chapter will examine the tactics elite teams employ against hostile armour and aircraft, and the variety weapons they can use for defence against these threats.

As Saddam Hussein discovered to his cost during the 1991 Gulf War, ground-based forces are very vulnerable against an enemy which has total air superiority. Iraqi ground units were subject to intense aerial attacks once the UN Coalition air units had swept their opponents from the skies. Iraqi ground forces suffered particularly badly once the ground war commenced on 24 February 1991.

Left: Milan in action. Note the wires attached to the rocket, which transmit guidance commands from the aimer throughout its flight.

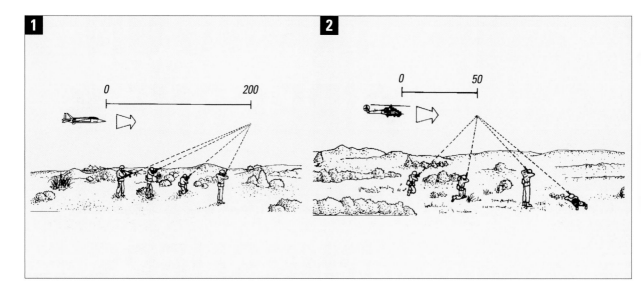

Above: Tactics for dealing with high-performance enemy aircraft (1). Machine-gun fire is directed 200m (656ft) in front of it to ensure a hit. With slower-moving helicopters (2) the distance comes down to a quarter of this.

The following is an extract from American Lieutenant-Colonel William Bryan, 2nd Battalion, 229th Aviation Regiment, who describes his unit of AH-64 Apache attack helicopters assaulting enemy units with rockets and cannon fire: 'On the fourth day of the ground war [28 February] we did a classic deep attack, moving about 300km [186 miles] towards Basra and intercepting one of the Republican Guard divisions as it attempted to withdraw north across the Euphrates. We used the same movement technique, attacking in three companies, but each company attacked in line, five abreast rather than as two teams. By that time there were so many oil well fires, and so many vehicles burning, that it was almost dark even though it was mid-afternoon. We had to use our FLIR [Forward Looking Infrared sensors] to see the targets, and even that was blanked out by smoke at 3000m [9750ft]. We called it "hell's half-acre". You could only see about 300m [970ft] with the naked eye.

'There were hundreds of vehicles in the column. This time we were fired on; we were engaged by several heat-seeking missiles, and we think some radar-guided SAM-6s were fired. It was like an inferno: there were so many fires and so much smoke that none of the enemy systems could acquire us. Most of what we fired at we hit, however. Visually, you could just see the flash of the explosions going off in the tunnel-like darkness, but through the FLIR the intense heat created by burning vehicles was easily visible.'

Anti-Aircraft Measures

For elite teams on the ground there are two methods of dealing with air attack: passive and active. Of the two, passive is much more desirable, because even if the aerial threat is dealt with, the presence of the team will be known to the enemy, and the mission may have been fatally compromised. Even unsophisticated aircraft may prove a major threat to special forces teams. During the Falklands War, for example, Argentinian Pucara ground-attack aircraft were considered such a threat to the proposed British landings at San Carlos that the SAS was sent in to destroy them, which was achieved in spectacular fashion on the night of 14/15 May.

The volume of fire from ground-attack aircraft can be massive. Flying as low as possible and at speeds of around 500kph (300mph), they open fire with cannon and machine gun fire at ranges of up to 1000m (3200ft) from the target. The machine guns or cannon fire at between 1000 and 4200 rounds per minute (the GAU-8 mounted on

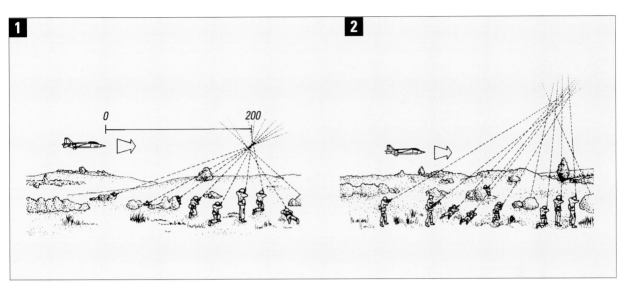

the A-10 Thunderbolt can fire at up to 4200 rounds per minute). The ground target is raked with fire, the area of impact moving along the ground with the speed of the aircraft. The cannons or guns can fire continuously for 30 seconds or more, covering a target 4000m (13,000ft) or over in length. To cover longer targets, such as troop columns, aircraft must attack in column formations, or by approaching abreast from a flank and then suddenly turning over a target. Helicopters, because of their hovering ability, can concentrate their fire at length in one attack against any part of a ground unit.

Because most aircraft machine guns and cannon are set at fixed lateral angles before take-off, their fire must be placed within narrow strips of ground for optimum results. One aircraft armed with eight machine guns firing a maximum of 4200 rounds in 30 seconds, for example, and flying over perfectly flat ground, will cover an area of 125,000 square metres (1,346,000 square feet) with its fire, and as the bullets strike the ground at a flat angle there will be a danger of ricochet. That said, there are a number of factors which will lessen the effectiveness of fire from aircraft directed at ground troops. First, ground irregularities will cause the fire to lift and scatter over a wide area. Second, the

minimum turning radius of even a light aircraft is several hundred metres, and thus sharp bends in the route being followed by ground troops will cause a halt in the firing.

Cluster Bombs

Fragmentation and cluster bombs dropped from aircraft are also a major threat to ground troops, particularly the latter. The cluster bomb, such as the American Rockeye, is a freefall weapon which consists of a thin-walled canister containing dozens of bomblets. A time or proximity fuse in the nose of the bomb activates a burster charge, which splits open the canister after release to disperse the bomblets over a wide area, thus compensating for the inherent inaccuracy of low-altitude bombing. The bomblets break into many fragments upon detonation, with each fragment travelling up to several hundred metres.

Faced with the above dangers, elite forces may seem hopelessly vulnerable. And they are, but only if they are discovered. Elite troops are trained in both passive and active anti-aircraft measures during their training, which gives them an excellent chance of both avoiding enemy aircraft and shooting them down when they have to. As mentioned above, passive measures are the most

Above: Against high-performance jets, small-arms fire should be concentrated to ensure a hit (1). A pre-arranged reference point (2) allows a ground team to place concentrated fire into the path of an incoming aircraft.

favoured form of anti-aircraft defence because they do not draw attention to the team on the ground. Passive measures are grouped under five headings: concealment, cover, dispersion, security and speed.

Prior planning will also aid staying hidden from enemy aircraft. Routes over rolling, broken and wooded ground should, if at all possible, be used as opposed to main highways or routes which have little cover. Concealment includes camouflage, making use of woods, taking advantage of darkness and poor visibility, limiting movements and using deception such as dummy installations and false lighting. During the 1991 Gulf War, American and British elite teams operating behind the lines in Iraq laid up during the day under camouflage netting to stay hidden from the Iraqi. Cover is used to minimise the effect of aerial ordnance. Cover can be provided by the terrain, by trenches and protective clothing. Unit dispersion reduces the effect of airborne weapons and also helps concealment, cover and security. In general, more casualties will be inflicted against a unit which is bunched up.

There are two elements to security measures. The first relates to the collection of intelligence regarding enemy air strengths and deployment. In this way the probability of an air attack can be determined. The second aspect concerns lookouts. Lookouts keep watch for enemy aircraft, paying particular attention to the direction of the sun, and to woods or any other cover which may screen the approach of low-flying aircraft. Lookouts should be equipped with binoculars and sun glasses and trained to recognise enemy aircraft. Lookouts should be relieved at least every 15 minutes. Speed is the final factor with regard to passive anti-aircraft measures. Put simply, an elite team should try to complete its mission as quickly as possible to reduce the amount of time it remains in enemy territory.

There may be occasions when teams will be caught out in the open. In this case the drill is clear: all soldiers seek any immediate cover and then open fire on the attacking aircraft. Ditches, gullies, trees and walls can offer protection to varying degrees from bomb fragments and machine-gun and

Right: Small-arms fire against aircraft flying directly at a team on the ground should be directed just above its nose for maximum effect.

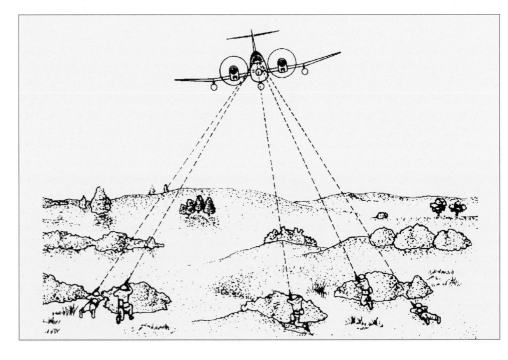

Left: Ground-attack aircraft such as this Harrier GR7 can do enormous damage to teams on the ground with their rockets, cannons and cluster bombs.

cannon fire. Ideally team members should take up positions 20-45 degrees off the aircraft's attack line and use burst fire along and in front of its line of flight. When an aircraft drops its bombs, all soldiers within the effective burst radius should cease firing and assume a prone position. Afterwards firing should be recommenced at any attacking aircraft still in range.

Against high-performance aircraft, such as jet fighters, small-arms fire should be directed 200m (650ft) or so in front of it to ensure hits. But the fire should be concentrated to guarantee at least some hits. Against helicopters, on the other hand, the distance is reduced to 50m (160ft). Sometimes it is easier to designate a reference point for a unit to place a concentrated fire pattern in the path of an approaching aircraft.

In defensive situations, the team should establish a position which has mutually supporting defensive fire, such as a ring of machine-gun positions. This ensures that enemy aircraft approaching from any direction run into a heavy volume of offensive fire before they arrive within bombing range. To be mutually supporting and give a uniformly effective firepower around the defended area, machine-gun units should be emplaced so their fire is not masked by obstacles.

With machine guns such as the British GPMG and American M60, fire is directed at the aircraft's nose; while it is flying past the weapon should be pointed well in front of its line of direction so that it flies into a wall of lead. Ideally, a 50-round controlled burst should be fired, the firer adjusting his fire by watching the tracer rounds (every four rounds in the belt should be tracer).

The Stinger

Because they are mostly lightly armed, elite teams will in the main only be able to employ small-arms fire against aircraft. However, vehicle-mounted teams, such as British SAS Land Rover columns in the Gulf War, were also equipped with Stinger man-portable SAMs. The Stinger gives elite forces a viable anti-aircraft weapon, and was used with great success against both aircraft and helicopters by the Afghan *Mujahedeen* during the war in Afghanistan. The Stinger's dimensions make it portable in theory, but the weight of other equipment carried by members of elite units really precludes it being employed by long-range foot patrols. The weapon is 1.53m (5ft) long and weighs 15.15kg (33.4lb). It consists of a missile in a sealed canister, a trigger assembly and an optical sight. The missile itself has a blunt

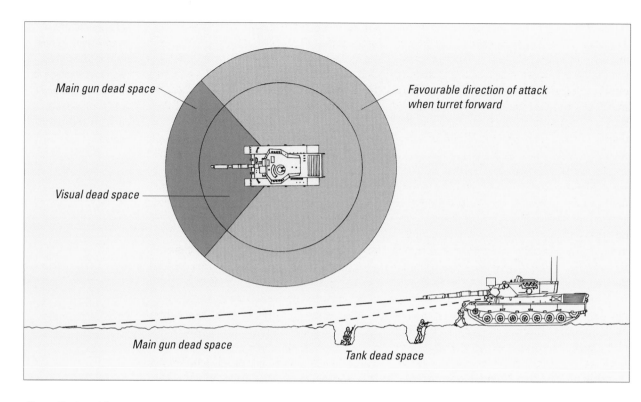

Main gun dead space

Favourable direction of attack
when turret forward

Visual dead space

Main gun dead space

Tank dead space

Above: Tanks with hatches closed have dead space of around 10m (33ft) to their front, and their main guns cannot be depressed to hit a target under 20m (66ft) away.

nose housing an infrared seeker, a cylindrical body and a tapered tail with four pop-out control canards and four folding tail fins. It is powered by a two-stage solid-fuel rocket motor and armed with a 3kg (6.6lb) high-explosive fragmentation warhead fitted with contact and proximity fuses. The missile's infrared seeker is resistant to flares and other basic infrared countermeasures, and the improved version, the Stinger-POST (Passive Optical Seeker Technology), gives better performance at very low altitudes.

When threatened with air attack, the operator simply places the launcher on his shoulder and acquires the target in his sight. If the Identification Friend or Foe (IFF) transponder indicates that the target is hostile, the operator must wait until the seeker achieves lock-on, as indicated by an audio tone. He then pulls the trigger. The small initial stage ejects the missile from the launch tube, before the main engine kicks in at a safe distance from the operator. The canards and tail fins then pop out, and the missile homes

automatically to the target. It does this by means of proportional navigation, whereby the guidance system steers the missile to achieve a constant line-of-sight between itself and the target.

Russia's Spetsnaz employs a similar man-portable SAM system called SA-14 'Gremlin'. It has a similar infrared seeker, which is believed to have enough sensitivity for all-aspect engagements, i.e. capable of attacking targets head-on and laterally, as opposed to rear-quarter only. Its warhead consists of 2.5kg (5.5lb) of high explosive, though overall it is considered inferior to the Stinger.

Though aircraft can pose a great threat to elite teams, standard operating procedures usually include strict rules of engagement with regard to shooting at aerial targets. This is to avoid friendly casualties, which in the confusion of battle frequently occur. Helicopters and light aircraft, for example, are not fired upon unless they have been positively identified. This is because they often fly around the battlefield without notifying headquarters as to their flight paths. The same goes for transport aircraft, which are only fired upon if they have been positively identified and are seen offloading enemy troops. In addition, aircraft usually make one or more passes for identification purposes before attacking, which gives the team more than one opportunity to fire.

The Armoured Threat

As well as the aerial threat, elite teams are likely to face enemy armoured vehicles at some time during their mission. These may be main battle tanks or, more likely, armoured personnel carriers (APCs), infantry fighting vehicles (IFVs) or armoured cars. To deal with these threats special forces troops need proper training regarding the vulnerable areas of armoured vehicles and appropriate weaponry. They also need something else, more intangible, as the French Foreign Legion's paratrooper manual states: 'Equipment and armament alone will not win battles. The morale factor must never be forgotten, and it is an important duty of all leaders to exercise their imagination and initiative toward inspiring their paratroops with a firm belief that they can defeat any form of tank attack.'

The first part of being able to defeat enemy armoured vehicles is to know their limitations and tactical doctrine. In this way an elite soldier or team can exploit their weaknesses. Tracked vehicles, especially tanks, can traverse shell holes, trenches and ditches, climb slopes and generally tackle difficult terrain within their spanning ability. The relatively low ground pressure of their tracks improves their ability to move across soft ground, which means they have the ability to outflank defensive positions. Because of their weight, main battle tanks can crush barbed wire defences, undergrowth, small trees, small buildings and men and their equipment. Their armour protection can withstand shell and bomb fragments, small-arms fire and some larger-calibre weapons.

But armoured vehicles do have weaknesses. Though they can traverse difficult terrain, their speed is greatly reduced in unfavourable conditions, such as steep slopes and areas covered by thick woods, swamps, jungles or boulders. The view of the crew is restricted, especially when all hatches and doors are closed. And this is further hampered by the pitching and rolling of the vehicle over uneven terrain. Armoured vehicles also tend to be 'deaf': the engine and track noises prevent their occupants from hearing external sounds.

Tank attacks are characterised by numbers launched with speed and violence, which literally punches a hole through the defences. They are accompanied by motorised infantry

Left: An example of what aircraft can do against an enemy caught in the open. These are Iraqi vehicles after being hit by United Nations aircraft during the 1991 Gulf War.

and artillery, with the vehicles spraying out a hail of machine-gun fire. Though this scenario is unlikely with regards to an attack against a small-sized elite team, even one tank and a few APCs present a major threat. Tactics for dealing with such an eventuality, like anti-aircraft measures, fall into two categories: active and passive. Active means are anti-tank weapons, which will be discussed below. Passive means include natural barriers, road blocks, buildings and demolitions.

The use of natural obstacles involves denying the enemy favourable routes of approach. This means making maximum use of any number of natural hindrances: unfordable water courses, marshes, thick jungle with large trees, large rocks, tree stumps, deep gullies and deep mud. Man-made obstacles can also be used to impede armoured vehicles: anti-tank trenches, large shell craters, canals, tank traps and mine fields. Elite teams will not normally be carrying mines because of bulk and weight considera-

Right: The American hand-held Stinger surface-to-air missile (SAM) system, which provides elite teams with a viable anti-aircraft defence.

tions, but there may be time to dig anti-tank trenches. These should have steep walls, with a width greater than half the length of the tank or vehicle they are intended to halt.

The principles of anti-tank action are to emplace and conceal the anti-tank weapons to meet the armoured attack and to hold up the attacking vehicles with obstacles to enable a clear shot. Standard infantry tactics involve anti-tank weapons placed in depth but this will not be possible with elite teams; rather, the anti-tank weapons will be used to give the team time to evacuate the area as quickly as possible. Where are the best locations to place anti-tank weapons? If possible, they should be sited on dead ground to conceal them from the enemy, ideally in defilade positions to hit an enemy from the flank. In addition, they can be placed on reverse slopes, ready to fire when the enemy vehicles crest the slope. In this way they will be safe from long-range tank or cannon fire until they can fire at the tanks' bellies when they cross the ridge line. Use can also be made of weather conditions. Though modern tanks are equipped with night-vision and thermal-imaging kit, they are still vulnerable in poor visibility and at night.

Anti-Tank Measures

As well as having to deal with armoured vehicles in the defence, elite teams may also be detailed to search them out and destroy them, for instance, before a major offensive. In this case the special forces team will try to attack at night. This is not only for concealment purposes: tanks usually rearm and refuel at night, either in a 'leaguer' (an administrative compound) or with a 'running replenishment' in the field. Either way, they will be bunched together, with little room to manoeuvre. As such they make ideal targets.

The thickness of armour on tanks and armoured vehicles varies on different parts of the hull. Tanks, for example, have their thickest armour at the front, with the thinnest armour on the side and underneath. This means that anti-tank rounds should be

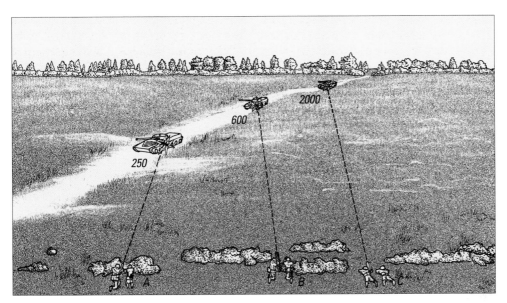

Left: Diagrammatic representation of the respective ranges (in metres) of the M72 (A), LAW 80 (B) and Milan (C) anti-tank systems. The increase in range is accompanied by a corresponding increase in equipment weight.

aimed at the side of the hull if possible. Tracks are vulnerable from any angle, but a disabled tank, usually known as a 'mobility kill', can still use its main and secondary armament. The turret and the glacis plate at the front of the tank is thick, and often invulnerable to hand-held anti-tank weapons. That said, a special forces soldier, if he has the courage, can approach a tank from the front to attack it. All tanks have dead space where the crew cannot observe the ground, and where the vehicle's weapons cannot be brought to bear. This is especially true when all the hatches are closed and the crew are entirely dependent on observation equipment to spot enemy infantry. This weakness can be exploited by firing rifles and machine guns at the vehicle to force the crew to 'close down'. A skilful soldier can then approach the tank from within the dead space and plant an explosive charge on its hull.

What of anti-tank weapons? For special forces patrols hand-held anti-tank weapons are ideal, being light yet powerful enough to knock out most armoured vehicles if used correctly. Of these, the American M72 66mm Light Anti-tank Weapon (LAW) is among the best. The system weighs 2.2kg (4.85lb) and is 878mm (34.2in) long when fully extended. It comes in a disposable launcher tube which serves as a protective package for the rocket and requires no maintenance. To fire the LAW, the front and rear covers are removed and the tube extended by grasping the backsight housing with one hand, holding the outer tube with the other, and then pulling back the backsight. Both sets of sights then spring up. On the backsight is a large aperture, the top of which is used in conjunction with the small tip on the foresight, which has a luminous spot. These are the battle sights for use at night or in poor weather conditions, and for quick aimed shots at targets up to 100m (320ft) away. There are two smaller apertures on the backsight that are marked either + degrees Centigrade or – degrees Centigrade. They are used in conjunction with the rest of the foresight according to the temperature conditions. For temperatures above freezing, for example, the lower aperture is used; for temperatures below freezing the upper is used. The foresight itself is constructed of clear plastic, and the ranges are represented by horizontal lines. The vertical central line is the aiming line, which is used against stationary, withdrawing or advancing targets. The outside vertical lines represent the amount of aim off needed to strike a target crossing at 25kph (16mph). The basic principles involved in firing at moving targets are as follows: targets which cross the line of sight at any angle are classified as crossing targets. In firing at targets which cross the line of sight the firer must aim ahead of the target so that the paths of the moving target and missile will meet. This taking aim ahead of the target is called the lead and is measured in target lengths. A medium-sized tank crossing the line of fire at right angles, or 90 degrees, at a speed of 5kph (3mph) at a range of over 200m (650ft) will require a third of a lead, and one lead if travelling at over 15kph (9mph).

To fire the LAW, the user checks the backblast danger area (the LAW has no recoil, but because the propellant gases escape to the rear of the launcher they will injure people standing directly behind up to a range of 8m/26ft) and ensures the sights are set at the proper temperature setting. The weapon is then shouldered so that the forehead is against the backsight. The safety catch is flicked off and then, after aim has been taken, the trigger is depressed with all the fingers on the right hand. The launcher can then be thrown away. A graphic example of

Below: The rocket of the M72 anti-tank weapon.

the LAW in use is provided by Chris Ryan, one of the members of the SAS team codenamed 'Bravo Two Zero', which was inserted behind Iraqi lines in the 1991 Gulf War. The group was attacked by Iraqi units, including armoured vehicles: 'Fifty metres, and they kept coming. Two Land-Rover-type vehicles, advancing at a purposeful crawl, obviously in search of me. I couldn't tell how many men they might contain. I held the sight of the 66 aligned between the front pair of lights. When they were some twenty metres off, I pulled the trigger.

'Whhoooosh! went the launcher, right in my ear. Out front there was a big BANG as the rocket took the vehicle head-on. Oddly enough, I remember no flash, just this heavy explosion, and a cloud of white smoke billowing out in the moonlight. The vehicle rolled to a stop.'

The LAW is capable of penetrating up to 260mm (10in) of armour. Larger anti-tank systems, such as the American Tube-launched, Optically tracked, Wire-guided (TOW) anti-tank missile and European Milan anti-tank system can penetrate up to 800mm (31in) and 1060mm (41in) of armour respectively. However, these are heavier – 28kg

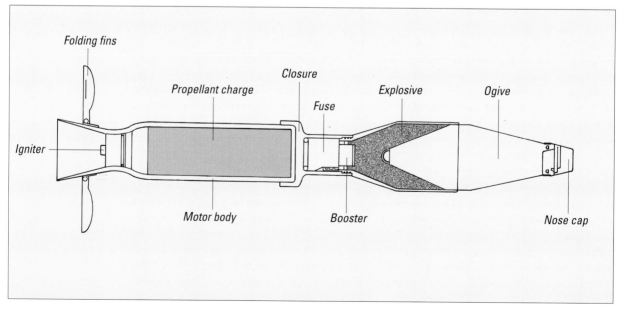

Folding fins

Closure

Propellant charge

Explosive

Ogive

Fuse

Igniter

Motor body

Booster

Nose cap

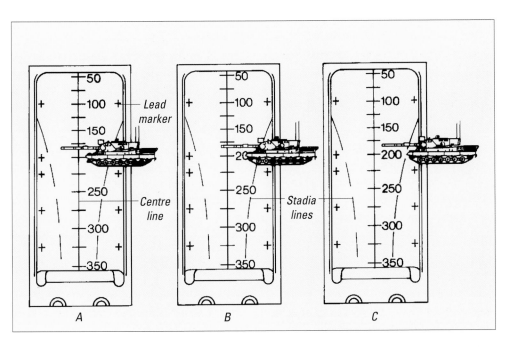

Left: The sights of the M72 LAW. The centre line is graded in metres. The artworks show when to fire the rocket when a tank is travelling at 5kph/3mph (A), 10kph/6mph (B) and 15kph/9mph (C).

(62lb) each – and more complicated to operate. During the 1991 Gulf War, British SAS Land Rovers mounted Milans as defence against Iraqi armour. To fire both systems, the aimer acquires the target in the crosshairs of the sight and pushes a firing button. The Semi-Active Command to Line-of-Sight (SACLOS) guidance system means the firer's control unit transmits commands to the missile via two thin copper wires which are paid out from a reel inside the missile. All the firer has to do is keep the target in the crosshairs until the missile impacts. Both systems have a very visible firing signature, and the wire guidance means firers have to remain in position until the missiles strikes its target.

Russia's Spetsnaz uses a similar system, the AT-4 'Spigot', which is similar to the Milan system, albeit inferior. Spigot is likewise controlled by wire guidance, and the operator must keep the target centred in his sight throughout the engagement. It can hit targets up to a rage of 2000m (6500ft), but, like its Western counterparts, the Spigot has several drawbacks: the long period of the missile's flight, the exposure of the operator to

counter-fire, the interruption of the line of sight by smoke or terrain masking and the degradation of its high-explosive warhead by modern composite and reactive armour.

Halfway between the TOW-type weapon and the LAW are the medium anti-tank weapons such as the British LAW 80. Capable of defeating tanks up to a range of 500m (1650ft), the LAW 80 is a one-shot throw-away device which can be used by elite teams. But it is heavier and more awkward than the M72, weighing around 10kg (22lb) and being 1m (3ft) long when retarded.

Probably the most widely-used of this class of weapon is the Russian RPG-7 series. The shoulder-launched RPG-7 has been in use since 1962, and has been a mainstay of infantrymen, guerrillas and elite forces ever since. The launcher is a simple tube with a venturi nozzle at the rear, some 950mm (37in) long and 7.9kg (17.4lb) in weight. A rocket-propelled 'grenade' projectile weighing another 2.5kg (5.5lb) is loaded at the muzzle, the larger diameter warhead of which protrudes from the front of the tube. There is normally an optical sight attached, although many users prefer the simple open

Above: Typical urban anti-tank firing positions. Cover must be used to aid an accurate first shot, after which the firer must move rapidly to another location as the weapon's signature will have alerted the enemy as to his whereabouts.

sights on the launcher tube. Passive night-vision sights can also be fitted.

When the projectile is loaded, the firer simply cocks the weapon by pulling down a cocking lever behind the main (front) grip. He puts the tube on this shoulder, holding the front and rear grips in his hands. He then aims, before pulling the trigger. The rocket ignites briefly, sending the projectile out of the tube and clear of the firer, before a second, sustainer charge burns. Firing creates a large backblast, giving the firer's position away, while forcing him to use a location with a clear area behind him. The RPG has a theoretical range of more than 500m (1625ft), but

most firers have difficulty in hitting a vehicle target at much above 300m (975ft). The projectile is extremely sensitive to crosswind, as the moving air presses against the finned tail section, causing the rocket motor to push the projectile into the wind. The warhead is a shaped-charge HEAT (High-Explosive Anti-Tank) type, and will penetrate the front armour of most APCs and light vehicles, and the side armour of all but the latest main battle tanks. It also has a powerful secondary effect, which makes the RPG-7 useful against bunkers, buildings and strongpoints. It has even been used successfully against helicopters, which are especially vulnerable when landing an assault force. The RPG is normally used by a two-man team, who carry up to eight reloads between them. Its effectiveness and reusability makes it popular with elite forces, especially the RPG-7D variant, which folds in two for carriage by paras and special forces. The larger-diameter RPG-16 (and RPG-16D 'folding version') is a later improved system, which fires a more powerful rocket which lies completely within the launcher tube. The RPG-18 and RPG-22 are Russian copies of the single-shot M72 LAW.

Like all infantry HEAT weapons, simple countermeasures can reduce their effectiveness. Armoured vehicles will travel in pairs, the machine guns of one providing cover to the other. Bounding overwatch tactics are also effective, where one vehicle remains static in a covering position while the other moves forward a short distance, then the two swap roles. Preventive fire can also be put down on cover such as bushes, buildings and ditches, all of which may conceal an RPG team. Simple screens of mesh or chains can be suspended a short distance from the vehicle's main armour – these cause premature detonation of an incoming warhead, greatly reducing its effectiveness. But notwithstanding, the RPG series is in use all around the world, and is highly regarded by conventional and elite forces as a handy, portable source of anti-tank and bunker-busting firepower.

For elite teams there are other, less sophisticated, anti-tank weapons available, though they have to be fashioned by materials to hand. These include grenades tied together and thrown at a tank track or under the vehicle, petrol thrown against tanks and set alight by incendiary bombs, or grenades and even steel bars thrust into track mechanisms. However, such measures are crude in the extreme and are used only in emergencies.

Left: An American Dragon anti-tank missile launcher. Developed in the 1960s, it was the first of a class of anti-tank weapons which were manportable, making them ideal for elite teams.

CHAPTER 15

SABOTAGE & BOOBY TRAPS

Sabotage is not simply a case of attaching explosives to targets and setting them off. It requires a specialist knowledge of how explosives react, placement theories and charge shapes. With booby traps, though, all that is required is a few simple materials and some imagination.

Special forces soldiers have always been trained in the use of explosives for the purposes of sabotage. To undertake successful sabotage missions requires an understanding of the types, characteristics and uses of explosives, proper placement of said charges on the target and the safe handling and storage of explosives in the target area. With this knowledge a small team can inflict major damage on an opponent. Sabotage operations usually involve the disruption of enemy supplies, services and industrial production. Targets include enemy communications centres, shipping, vehicles, bridges, roads, railway lines, telephone exchanges, power stations and supply depots. But before these targets can be destroyed, an elite soldier has to choose the right type of explosive.

Explosives are defined as substances that violently change due to a chemical reaction, and release pressure and heat equally in all directions. They are classified as high or low explosives according to the detonating velocity or speed at which this change takes place. Low explosives change, or deflagrate, from a solid to a

Left: Spectacular explosions do not necessarily mean successful sabotage. More important are the right explosives and their correct use.

Right: The solid black rectangles indicate where charges should be placed to demolish a slab bridge, i.e. underneath the span.

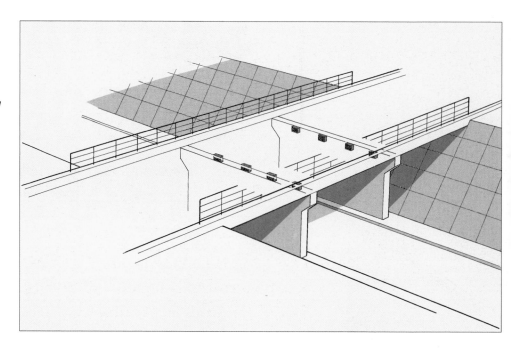

gaseous state relatively slowly over a sustained period – at 400mps (1312fps). An example of a low explosive is black powder. High explosives change into a gaseous state at a much higher rate – up to 8500mps (27,600fps) – producing a shattering effect upon the target. This shattering effect is highly desirable in military explosives, and is used in shells, bombs and mines, and also for sabotage purposes.

Explosives vary not only in their detonating rate or velocity, but also in factors such as density and heat production, which determine their effectiveness. They vary so much that the amount of explosive used is computed according to a relative effectiveness factor, with the effectiveness of Trinitrotoluene (TNT) taken as the base value. The latter, with a detonating velocity of 7010mps (23,000fps), has a relative effectiveness factor of one, while Tetrytol, with the same velocity, has a relative effectiveness factor of 1.2. For military sabotage missions, explosives need to have certain characteristics, these are: relative insensitivity to shock or friction, a detonating velocity that is adequate for the purpose, high power per unit of weight, a

high density, stability under different temperatures, detonation by easily prepared primers, convenient shape for storage and packaging, and a long shelf life.

The most popular types of high explosives for sabotage operations are TNT, Tetrytol, Composition C3 and C4 (plastic explosive), Semtex, PE4 and Amatol. But these explosives will not detonate without firing systems. It may be surprising to know, but TNT can be hit with a hammer and it will not detonate, not without a firing system.

There are two types of firing system: electrical and non-electrical. A non-electrical firing system is an explosive charge prepared for detonation by means of a non-electrical blasting cap – a thin tube 250mm (9in) long - which is embedded in the explosive charge. The blasting cap provides the detonating impulse required to ignite the charge. The fuse itself can either be a safety fuse or detonating cord. The former consists of flexible cord around 5mm (0.2in) in diameter which consists of black powder encased in a fibre wrapping, which itself is covered in a waterproof material. When this fuse has been lit by a flame it burns at a rate of 8mm (0.3in)

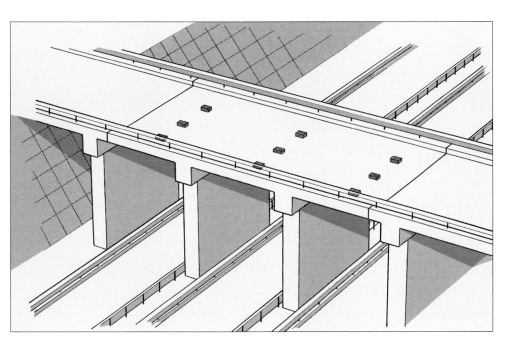

Left: Placement of charges on a concrete cantilever bride. The bridge is demolished by destroying the cantilever action and unbalancing the cantilever arms.

per second. Detonating cord consists of a small explosive core well protected by up to six layers of material, which detonates at a rapid rate of 6000-8000mps (19,500-26,000fps). The detonating cord itself is detonated by a detonator.

In electrical firing systems, the blasting cap contains two wires which are connected in the cap by a bridge wire. When a current is passed through the wires this bridge wire becomes hot and ignites the charge within the cap, thus detonating the main explosive charge. The charges themselves can be set off in one of three ways: by a soldier lighting a fuse or detonating a charge nearby, by means of a timer, whereby the charge detonates after a pre-set interval, or detonation by remote control.

The correct placement of explosive charges on a target is absolutely crucial to sabotage operations. The charges should be placed at the position which will provide maximum effectiveness. For the purposes of cratering, for example, they are placed in

Below: A cantilever bridge destroyed by Serb sabotage in Bosnia during the inter-ethnic strife which took place in the mid-1990s (and temporarily repaired courtesy of the British Army).

Right: To destroy a reinforced concrete open spandrel arch bridge, the charges (in solid black) are placed as shown.

holes in the ground; for cutting timber they are tied to the outside of the tree or placed in boreholes. The charges may be fastened to the target by wire, adhesive tape, or propped against the target by means of wooden or metal frames. As to the size of the charge required to do the job, it is calculated by formula based on its effectiveness in relation to that of TNT. For purposes of simplification, the amount of explosive required to cut a tree of 76cm (30in) diameter using an untamped (uncovered) external charge is 10.2kg (22.5lb) of TNT. The charge itself will be placed as close as possible to the surface of the tree, and experts usually notch the tree to hold the charge in place. If the tree is not round and the direction of fall does not matter, the charge will be placed on the widest face so that the cut will be through the least thickness. In this way the tree will fall towards the side where the charge is placed, unless unduly influenced by wind or lean. To ensure the tree falls in the right direction, a so-called kicker charge of 0.45kg (1lb) of TNT can be placed two-thirds of the distance up the tree on the opposite side. For internal charges when cutting timber, the explosives are placed in boreholes parallel to the great-

est dimension of cross section and tightly covered with moist clay or sand. Two boreholes can be used to cut rounded timber, with the charges at right angles to each other. Charges placed at a height of 1.5m (5ft) above ground level will leave stumps that are difficult to remove, thus creating a hindrance to the enemy (not all trees will be blown to harm the opposition; during jungle operations, for example, clearances may be made to facilitate helicopter medical evacuation).

Elite demolitions experts will also have to have a knowledge of how to cut steel, which appears in bridge construction, railway lines, armoured vehicles, ships hulls and a host of other military equipment. As mentioned above, when high explosive detonates, the explosive changes violently from a solid into compressed gas at very high pressure. This rate of change is determined by the type of explosive and the density, confinement and size of the charge. This detonation produces a shock wave of tremendous pressure that, although lasting only a few microseconds, can shatter and displace objects in its path as it travels from its point of origin. This shock wave is transmitted to any object in contact with the explosive.

Left: British troops after crossing the Rhine in March 1943, at the end of World War II. Note the sabotaged bridge in the background.

When detonated in direct contact with a steel plate, a high-explosive charge produces an indentation or depression with an area about the size of the contact area of the explosive charge. Directly opposite the explosive charge a slab of metal will be torn from the other surface of the plate; this is approximately the shape of the explosive charge, though its area is greater than that of the contact area. The steel will be split under the exploded charge along its entire length, with a cross fracture being formed across the end of the charge away from the point of detonation. The force of an explosion is proportional to the quantity and power of the explosive charge, but the destructive power depends

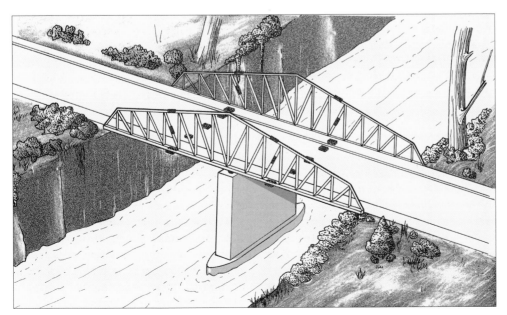

Left: Placement of explosive charges to destroy a continuous span truss bridge. The charges cause the bridge to become unbalanced, after which it will collapse.

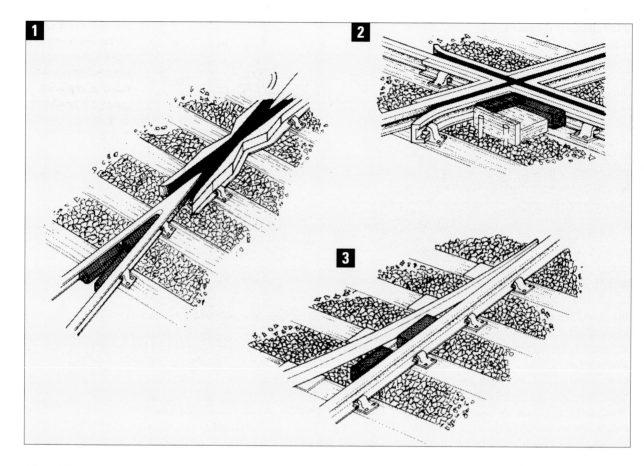

Above: When sabotaging railways, elite teams will try to place explosives on frogs (1), crossovers (2) and switches (3) to disrupt two lines at once.

on the contact between the explosive and the target, and on the manner in which the explosive is directed at the target. For maximum effect against steel, an explosive charge the correct shape and size for the intended target must be detonated in close contact with the steel along the desired line of cut. This close contact is essential, as any water or air gap between the charge and steel will reduce the cutting effect. In addition, the charge must be of a certain thickness, because if it is spread too thinly there will be insufficient space for the detonation to attain full velocity before striking the target. If this is the case the shock wave will travel parallel to the surface, and the volume of the target will be too much for the strength of the shock wave – a waste of explosive.

There is also a problem with charges that are too thick. In this case the contact area will be narrow and the shock wave will be transmitted over too little of the target area, resulting in excessive lateral loss of energy. Military specialists have worked out that the best ratio of charge width to charge thickness is three to one for contact charges placed on steel structures up to 7.6cm (3in) thick.

Of course, the special forces demolition expert will not only have to cut steel beams, he will also have to blow up bridges and similar structures. In this case he will try and use breaching charges. Again the size, placement, tamping and confinement of the charge is very important, particularly the size and confinement. High-explosive breaching charges, detonated in or against concrete and rock, must produce a shock so intense that it shatters or breaks the material. In general, the breaching radius for internal charges is half the thickness of the mass to be breached if the charge is placed midway into the mass. If holes are drilled less than halfway into the mass, the breaching radius becomes the longer distance from the end of the hole to the outside of the mass. Thus the breaching of a 1.2m (4ft) wall by an internal charge placed 0.3m (1ft) into the mass will produce a breaching radius of 1m (3ft). If the wall is to be breached by a centred internal charge, the breaching radius is 0.6m (2ft). The breaching radius is 1.2m (4ft) if an external charge is used.

Placement of Charges

As with steel, the placement of explosive charges on concrete and stone is very important. In the demolition of piers and walls, the positions for the placement of charges are limited. Unless a demolition chamber is available, the charges have to be placed against one face of the target at ground level, above ground level or beneath the surface. A charge above ground level is more effective than one placed directly on the ground. When several charges are required to destroy a concrete or stone structure, the charges are placed equally at no less than one breaching radius high from the base of the target. This configuration makes the best use of the shock waves from the blast. Ideally, all the charges should be covered with damp sand or sandbags if there is time.

One of the priority targets for elite teams operating behind the lines will be enemy lines of supply, specifically railway lines and bridges. The amount of demolition will be determined by target requirements. For example, bridges are generally demolished to create obstacles that delay the enemy. In this case the delay can be obtained by blasting a gap too long to be spanned by the enemy's bridging equipment. Bridges which are large may require large amounts of explosive. In this case the team will be governed by several factors before demolition takes place. First, the tactical and strategic situation that indicates the length of time the enemy must be delayed, the time available for demolition,

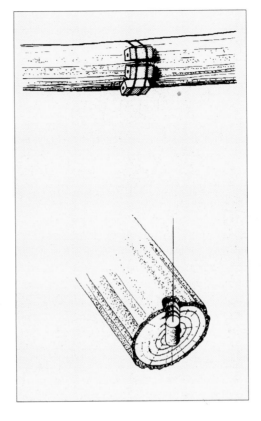

Left: **When cutting timber, the charges can be either wrapped around the tree (top) or placed inside it in boreholes (bottom).**

and the extent of denial to be accomplished. Second, the likelihood that friendly forces may occupy the area and require use of the bridge. Third, the results to be gained by the expenditure of time and materials compared to the results that can be achieved against another target with the same effort. Fourth, the manpower, equipment and quantities of explosives available.

For the purposes of military demolitions, bridges are divided into two main sections: the lower part (substructure) and the upper part (superstructure). The lower part consists of the supports for the upper part, and in the main are end supports or abutments, and intermediate supports or piers. Abutments and piers may be made of steel, iron, concrete, masonry or timber. The upper part of a bridge, the superstructure, includes the flooring, stringers, floor beams and any girders that make up the total part of the bridge above the substructure.

Demolishing bridges calls for careful planning. The size and placement of the charges will depend on the characteristics of the individual bridge to be demolished. That said, there are some general procedures that have to be followed. First, some charges may be laid quickly, in case the enemy interrupts the team before the demolition is fully prepared. If possible, these ought to be placed so that they may be included later on in the deliberate demolition of the bridge. Second, it may be possible to economise on the use of explosives by blasting several times rather than only once. If this is possible it should be done. Third, tension beams or supports on bridges are always more difficult to repair than compression beams or supports. They should therefore be given priority. Fourth, the destruction of bridges over canals or railways should be planned so that any temporary piers that may be erected later by the enemy will interfere with the traffic on the canal or railway. Fifth, any long steel beams that require cutting in only one place to demolish the bridge should be further damaged to prevent their later salvage. Sixth, the nature of the terrain under the bridge is of great importance to the success of the demolition. For example, blowing a bridge over a river or gorge which has no supporting piers at each end will mean the weight of the bridge will cause it to fall.

One of the most common bridges in the world is the stringer bridge, whereby steel or masonry stringers run longitudinally with the bridge and directly support the deck. In simple span bridges the stringers extend only from one support to the next. To blow this type of bridge the explosives will be placed so that they cut the stringers. With concrete slab bridges the charges must be place to ensure the dropping of a slab. With a concrete cantilever bridge, whereby the construction joints are in the span but not over the piers, the superstructure can be demolished by cutting each cantilever arm adjacent to the suspended span. If a large gap is the object, the cantilever arms should be cut in such a way as to drop the cantilever arms and the suspended spans.

With truss bridges – a jointed frame structure consisting of straight steel or timber supports either above and each side of the deck or laid below the roadway – the aim is to cut the upper and lower chords at both ends of one truss in each span on the upstream side. If this happens the bridge will roll over, thereby twisting the other truss off its sup-

Right: A simple grenade booby trap. The tripwire extracts the grenade's pin when forced forward by the victim's leg.

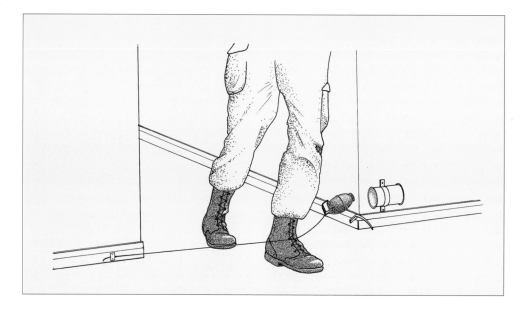

Left: Western Allied vehicles parked during the 1991 Gulf War against Iraq. Such concentrations are ideal targets for elite sabotage teams, as they allow the single explosive charges to destroy more than one target at once.

port. With a continuous span truss bridge, where the span trusses are extended over two spans, the heaviest chord sections and the greatest depth of truss are located over the intermediate supports; again the charges should be placed so that the bridge becomes unbalanced and collapses.

Suspension span bridges, such as San Francisco's Golden Gate and the Humber Bridge in Britain, present major challenges with regard to demolitions. This type of bridge is usually distinguished by two characteristics: the roadway is carried by a flexible member and the spans are long. It will have several components: suspension cables which are usually two steel multi-wired members that pass over the tops of towers to anchorages on each bank; these cables are the load-carrying members. The aforementioned Golden Gate, for example, has 204,300km (127,000 miles) of cable wire. The towers of a suspension bridge support the cables or load-carrying members. They are usually made of steel, concrete masonry or a combination of these materials. The trusses

or girders of suspension bridges do not support the load directly: they provide only stiffening. Anchorage consists of setting the splayed end of the cable in a rock or a concrete mass.

Suspension span bridges can be attacked at several points. The towers and anchorages are usually too large to be destroyed, and the

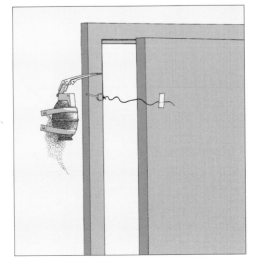

Left: A variation of the grenade booby trap. Opening the door pushes the tripwire forward and pulls the grenade's pin.

Above: A simplified illustrated of a booby trapped helicopter landing zone (LZ). Each pole has a grenade fitted to it, the pin of which is connected via a trip-wire to another pole-mounted grenade across the LZ. When the helicopter lands it detonates the grenades.

cables are usually too thick to be cut with charges. The best method of destruction is either by dropping the span leading onto the bridge or dropping a section of the roadway by cutting the suspenders from the main or load-bearing cables. The length of this section should be determined by an analysis of the capabilities the enemy has for repair. With a smaller suspension bridge, the towers and cables are vulnerable. Charges may be placed on the towers slightly above the roadway. Cables can also be cut by placing the charges as close as possible to either the top of a tower or an anchorage. However, cables can be difficult to cut because of the air space between the individual wires.

As well as bridges, railways are a prime target for elite teams. It is difficult for an enemy to safeguard the whole of his railway network, which means teams can cut lines at several points. Blowing a length of track is easy, but really a waste of explosives. Charges should be placed at vulnerable points such as curves, switches and crossovers, which will interfere with two or more lines. If possible, the team will aim to destroy a railway tunnel, especially if it is located on a major route to strategic military or industrial areas. However, tunnel demolition usually requires large amounts of explosive, though this can be reduced somewhat with carefully prepared charges and placement. The most important factor in tunnel demolition is the tightness of the lining against solid rock. The degree of contact of the walls with surrounding rock influences the amount of blast energy transmitted to the rock or retained in the concrete and the subsequent movement of broken fragments.

If a team has time, it will be able to destroy a tunnel with charges detonated in prepared chambers in the material adjacent to the inner face of the tunnel. These chambers can face each other at staggered intervals. Each chamber should be no more that 1m (3ft) wide and 1.2m (4ft) high, and at least 9m (30ft) into the tunnel to ensure confinement of the charge.

Rear area airfields and depots will also be targets for demolition teams, in particular enemy tanks and aircraft. These targets can easily be put out of action with a few kilos of carefully placed charges. Tanks, for example, can be disabled by charges placed on their tracks, on top of the engine compartment or under the turret, which can damage the turret ring. Modern military aircraft are stuffed full of sophisticated avionics, which can be damaged by small charges placed on nose cones, in cockpits and just behind the cockpit. In addition, charges placed on undercarriages, exhaust turbines and air intakes can also put them out of action.

The Saddle Charge

Much of the techniques above involve the proper placement of charges. Elite teams will have this knowledge, but they will also have the expertise to build advanced charges made of plastic explosives to destroy targets more effectively. The saddle charge, for example, is used for cutting steel bars up to 20cm (8in) in diameter, which will include engine turbines and propellers. The charge consists of explosive formed into a triangular shape, with the base being half the circumference of the target. The long axis is twice the length of the base, and the charge is primed at the apex of the triangle. The saddle charge works by using a so-called cross fracture: the fracture forms below the base of this triangular-shaped charge and cuts the steel.

The diamond charge is used for targets similar to those which the saddle charge is used. When detonated, the shock waves, meeting in the centre of the charge, are deflected at right angles, cutting down into the target. The explosive is formed into the shape of a diamond and then wrapped around the target, the layer ensuring that both ends of the long axis touch. To give some idea of the power of the diamond charge, 5mm (0.2in) of explosive is all that is required to cut 20mm (0.8in) of mild steel.

The principle of counter force is also used by special forces teams, especially against dense concrete up to 1.2m (4ft) thick. The simultaneous detonation of two diametrically opposed charges on a target causes the shock waves to meet in the target's centre, resulting in massive internal pressures and damage. The actual size of the charge will be determined by the thickness of the target to be breached. To determine this, the commander will obey a standard formula: multiply the diameter or thickness of the target to be breached by five, which gives the amount in pounds of plastic explosive required for reinforced concrete. The amount of explosive required is then divided in half and the two charges placed diametrically opposite to one another on the target. Both sides of the target must be accessible. Once in place both charges must be detonated simultaneously to ensure maximum force.

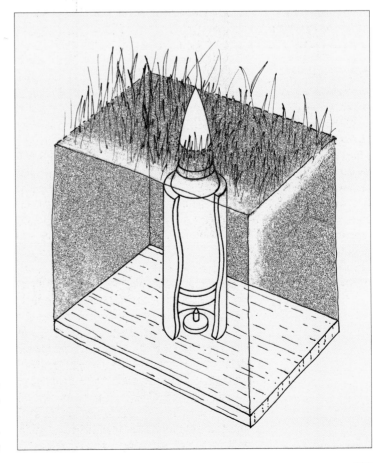

Below: The simple cartridge trap. A bullet is buried in the earth resting on a pin. When stepped on t he bullet goes off, blowing off the victim's foot.

In general, a shaped charge is designed to concentrate the energy of the explosion into a small area to make a tubular or linear fracture in the material on which it is placed. It is extremely effective against steel and concrete and can also be easily improvised. For example, almost any conically shaped container can be used to make a shaped charge: cups, bowls, wine bottles and cocktail glasses. Even if no vessel is available, by simply cutting a cavity into a block of plastic explosive a special forces soldier can create a shaped charge. In general, the following principles apply when constructing improvised shaped charges: the angle of the cone should be between 30-60 degrees; the stand-off distance (the distance from the bottom of the shaped charge to the target) should be 1-2 times the diameter of the cone; the height of the explosive measured from the base of the cone should be twice the height of the cone; the point of detonation should be exactly top centre; and an ogive (curved profile) must be used if the charge is placed underwater.

Special forces soldiers are fully trained in the use of explosives in booby traps, though the possession of explosives is not a prerequisite for constructing effective booby traps. A booby trap is designed to cause sudden and unexpected casualties, which will result in reduced enemy morale by creating fear, suspicion and uncertainty. In this way an elite team can slow down an enemy pursuing force to expedite its escape, or generally sow confusion in enemy areas. An American who fought in Vietnam, Leroy Thompson, provides a good example of the thoughts of the foot soldier when faced with booby traps: 'Vietnam was a very nasty war and booby traps were one of its nastier aspects. They scared the hell out of me. The thought of my leg being punctured by a faeces-smeared spike and turning gangrenous frequently crept into my mind as I moved through the boonies. I was extremely cautious and paid attention to every booby trap update that came down the turnpike ... Fear is the primary result of a booby trap campaign. Seeing a bloody stump where a buddy's foot had been blown off, or his torso punctured by the spikes of a bamboo whip, sapped the morale of the US troops.'

Below: Booby trapped mines. In 1, when the mine is lifted the wire fixed to the stake sets off the activator. In 2, the bottom mine is booby trapped by the top one. Lifting the top mine out activates the firing device fitted to the one underneath.

Simple Booby Traps

The simplest booby traps are often the most effective. A simple grenade fastened to a post or tree with its pin attached to a tripwire can be very effective. Usually secured across a path or trail; when an enemy soldier inadvertently walks into the tripwire the pin is pulled and the grenade is detonated. In addition, grenades can be used to booby trap gates. The grenade is buried shallowly and a short tripwire attached to the bottom of the gate – the slightest movement of the gate is enough to detonate the grenade under a victim's feet. Grenades can also be used to devastating effect against incoming helicopters. During the Vietnam War, for example, Viet Cong guerrillas would booby trap

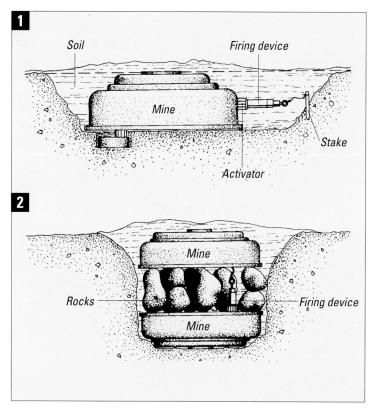

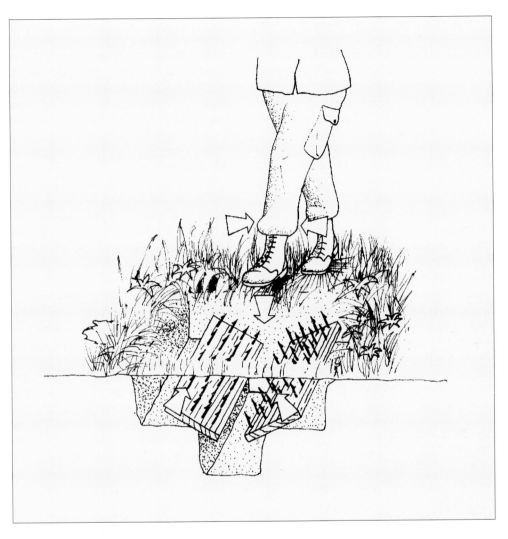

Left: The punji bear trap. The two boards with spikes driven through them pivot when stepped on, forcing the spikes through the calf.

Below: The bridge trap. The boards on the bridge are sawed through, with spikes placed underneath. When stepped on, the boards give way and the victim is impaled on the spikes.

potential landing sites (there is a limited number of landing sites in the jungle). This consisted of at least four bamboo poles, attached to the top of which were grenades. The ends of each tripwire were attached to rings of a grenade, with the tripwires strung across the landing site. When the helicopter came in to land it would snare the tripwires, setting off the grenades.

The rules concerning the planting of booby traps are quite simple. First, all traps should be camouflaged as much as possible. Second, they should be located in a position that channels the enemy into the booby trapped area, such as a defile, room or

tunnel. Third, traps should be laid in groups so that when an enemy force comes across them it is likely to spring at least one. Among these traps should be one dummy booby trap. When this is discovered and found to be harmless, it may lull an unwary enemy into a false sense of security. Fourth, booby traps should be placed on obstacles, the removal of which sets the trap off. Weapons, food and general supplies can also be booby trapped: when they are picked up the booby traps will be initiated.

Even without grenades or other ordnance, elite teams can construct potentially fatal traps. A simple piece of wood with nails or spikes driven through it and left in a hole in the ground with the spikes pointing up is a vicious trap. It can be positioned almost anywhere, being difficult to spot until it has been stepped on. In addition, the spikes can be tipped with poison or excrement. Spikes can also be placed on the grass on the banks of gullies or streams, so that anyone jumping from one bank to another will impale themselves. American troops in Vietnam soon learned to counter this type of trap by wearing steel boot inserts. However, the Viet Cong (VC) soon countered this with one of the oldest booby traps around: the punji bear trap. Concealed under brushwood or leaves on a track, it consisted of two boards or steel plates with spikes driven through them. These boards were designed to pivot when stepped on and drive the spikes into the unprotected area of the calf above the boot.

Booby trapping tunnels was a speciality of the VC. These included placing spikes or stakes at the entrance, and even mining the entrance with command-detonated grenades. They had other tunnel defences, as Leroy Thompson states: 'But the most diabolical booby trap of all was at the entrance where the [American] tunnel rat would have to hang by his hands from the edge before dropping into the tunnel. There would be a slit at eye level. Through it, a spear would be driven into the face of the victim by a waiting VC or a tripwire arrangement.' Other spike traps include the bridge trap. This is an ingenious little trap which catches the unwary. A local bridge is sawed through to make a hole, underneath which are stakes concealed by

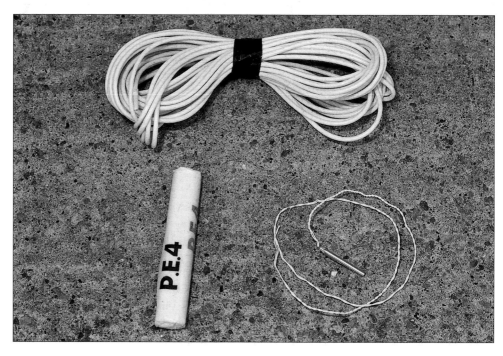

Right: PE4 plastic explosive, detonating cord (top) and an electrical detonator, as used by Western elite teams.

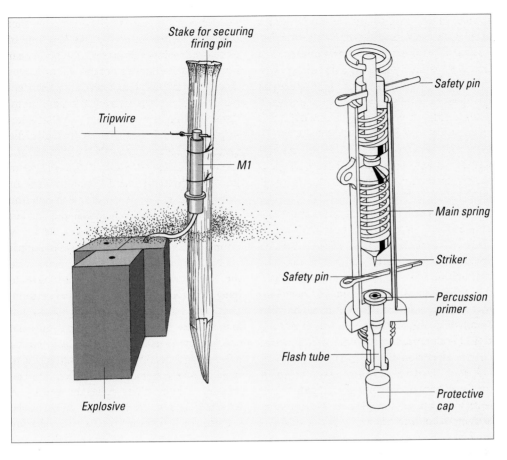

Stake for securing firing pin

Tripwire

M1

Explosive

Safety pin

Main spring

Striker

Safety pin

Percussion primer

Flash tube

Protective cap

Left: A booby trap using the American M1 pull-firing device. The M1 sets off the explosive when the wire is tripped.

the water of a drainage ditch. The hole is camouflaged so that it is indistinct from the rest of the bridge's surface. When stepped on, though, the unfortunate victim's leg goes through the camouflage and gets impaled on the stakes.

If the team has grenades or bullets to hand it can lay them to trap pursuing forces. One of the simplest booby traps is the cartridge trap. This consists of a round buried in the ground so that only the head is partially exposed. Pressure applied to the head, i.e. a foot stepping on it, forces it farther into the ground. But the round is resting on a pin or spike, which fires the round into the foot – very simple and very effective. The overhead grenade trap consists of a grenade suspended in foliage overhead, with its pin running down to a tripwire. When the wire is tripped the pin is extracted and, three to five seconds

later, anyone below is showered with shrapnel. Because it is hanging overhead, the blast radius of the grenade is increased.

American Special Forces, SEALs and Rangers are equipped with firing devices which have designations M1 to M5. These devices can be used to set booby traps. The M1, for example, is a delaying device, which contains acid to eat through the restraining wire in a predetermined time – eight to 15 seconds – after which a powerful spring drives a firing pin into primer explosive. The resultant explosion is channelled through the mouth of the device into plastic explosive. The ampoule of acid can be crushed by attaching the M1's locking safety pin to a tripwire, making for a very effective booby trap. The M2 weatherproof lighter can even be used underwater. A pull on the striker retaining pin causes the striker to hit the primer,

Right: A simple grenade booby trap in the field. This sort of device can inflict many injuries on a pursuing team.

igniting the fuse. During the Falklands War, the Argentinians made a number of booby traps using American M1 pull-firing devices and blocks of TNT. The latter would be buried underground, with a detonator inserted in it connected to an M1 firing device. The M1 would be fastened to a stake, which in turn was attached to a tripwire. When the wire was tripped the M1's safety pin was extracted, setting in train the explosive sequence.

Other explosive booby traps include the so-called vehicle rut trap. This trap is used to blow up vehicles, and consists of a hole dug in a rut in the road. In the hole is placed a grenade with its firing pin attached to a tripwire. Around the grenade is placed enough explosive sufficient to disable or destroy the target vehicle. The other end of the tripwire is attached to a stake on the other side of the hole, and the wire should be taut. The hole is then covered with tarpaulin or sacking, supported by some sort of improvised frame. Whatever the method, it should blend in with the road so the driver is unsuspecting. When the vehicle drives over the hole the wheel falls into the hole and applies pressure to the tripwire, which detonates the grenade and the explosive around it. It would take a great deal of explosive to destroy a tank, but booby traps can be designed to injure tank crews and any enemy infantry riding on their hulls.

Two poles can be positioned either side of a road or track, with a wire stretched over the road and attached to the top of the poles. Two grenades are then fastened to this wire, each one approximately a third of the way across from each pole. Their pins are attached to wires which run to stakes driven into the ground. The whole trap should be positioned within foliage so that it can be adequately camouflaged. When the tank rumbles through it pushes the wire attached to the two poles forward, causing the pins to be pulled from the grenades and detonating them. Two or more grenades can be used, and as well as tanks this trap is very effective against trucks carrying infantry.

Spear traps have been used for centuries as a way of trapping animals for food, but they can also be used against human prey. In the main they consist of a springy shaft which is held in place by a tripwire, with a spear or stake being firmly lashed to the springy shaft. When the tripwire is sprung the springy shaft is released, sending the spear or stake into the victim. These types of booby traps can inflict nasty injuries. And booby traps do not necessarily have to kill. Leroy Thompson should have the final words: 'Since VC medical facilities were primitive, we actually preferred a seriously injured VC to a dead one, as it put more of a strain on their limited resources'.

INDEX